The Exceptionally Human Airport Experience

Brian Shapiro

Shapiro Communications Publishing
2018

Copyright (c) 2018 by Brian Shapiro

All rights reserved. This book or any portion thereof may not be reproduced or used in any manner whatsoever without the express written permission of the publisher except for the use of brief quotations in a book review or scholarly journal.

First Printing: 2018

ISBN: 978-0-9972848-2-9

Shapiro Communications Publishing
245 S. 16th Street
Philadelphia, PA 19102

www.shapirocommunications.com

Acknowledgments

First, I would like to thank the dedicated professionals in the airport community who do their best to create outstanding experiences under extraordinarily challenging circumstances. Your tireless efforts are not without notice. It is a pleasure to try and bring some additional value to the tremendous work you are already doing. A giant thank you to all those on the airport front line, as you are the people who bring that human touch to the travelers. You have no easy task, and more often than not, you do it exceedingly well. A special thanks to everyone at my hometown airport, Philadelphia International (PHL), for their ongoing dedication to enhancing the airport experience. I want to thank my editors, Peter McEllhenney and Nora Foreshcle. Peter, your ability to transform raw material into a coherent structure is truly exceptional. Nora, your sudden and unexpected passing just days after completing your editing work is deeply felt. Your mastery of grammar and sentence structure allowed people like myself to actually bring books to life. May your family find some peace knowing your work on this book will help bring an increasingly human touch to countless airport interactions worldwide. Thank you to Rebekah Rius at Sidecar Solutions for your work on the book cover as well as your marketing support. Special thanks to Danette Wilson, who has been with Shapiro Communications since the start and who has made countless contributions to our growth and success. Finally, I want to thank my wife Adina, for her unwavering support, and our sons Asa and Levi, for their love of travel keeps us returning to airports on a semi-regular basis.

Forward

"Airports frequently measure customer satisfaction in relation to functional aspects such as passenger processes, airport facilities and customer services; however, the emotional aspects of the customer experience are rarely measured, if at all."
-Karla Straker and Cara Wrigley

Customer experience is everywhere in business these days, but sometimes we forget it starts from inside of the company, with our employees. Indeed, when we manage a customer experience program, it is crucial to have an outside-in perspective. But to deploy it, we must rely on our internal resources and staff.

In 2016, ACI World demonstrated that customer experience is usually the best way to increase non-aeronautical revenues (NAR) through the research paper "Does passenger satisfaction increase airport non-aeronautical revenues?" According to this study, three variables impact non-aeronautical revenues:

- An increase of 1 percent in the number of passengers leads to a growth of NAR ranging from 0.7 percent to 1 percent;
- An increase of 1 percent in the size of the commercial area leads to a growth of NAR of 0.2 percent;
- An increase of 1 percent in the global passenger satisfaction mean (as defined in Airport Service Quality - ASQ survey) generates, on average, a growth of NAR of 1.5 percent.

Customer experience management provides the best ROI in the airport industry, but it's also a very complex business, with a lot of people involved from different airport teams and other stakeholders such as airlines, retailers, governments and more. Furthermore, an airport is often a place with passengers coming from different countries and cultures, and consequently with different expectations about what they need as service and how they define a delightful and memorable experience in an airport. When we interact with someone, it is crucial to adapt our communication style to her background.

According to the Harvard Business Review, "customer experience can be defined as the sum of all interactions a customer has with a company or an entity providing a paid service. This can include everything from a customer's initial awareness or discovery of a company, product or service, through the purchase and use of that company's products or services." These interactions can be delivered in person, through the Internet or through other channels. Together, these all add up to the critical moments—what we call touch points or moments of truth—that create an organization's overall customer experience.

Forrester Research suggests that there is convergence between customer experience and human experience, and customer experience is mainly driven by emotions. Even if there are more and more self-services and technology in airports, and these technical innovations contribute to enhancing the overall service, the human touch is still an important driver that needs to be considered for customer satisfaction.

Fundamentally, customer experience is an encounter between two people. This is why a concept called "symmetry of attention" is crucial. Symmetry of attention can best be described as follows: If you keep your employees happy, the employees will keep your customers happy. You can also treat and consider your employees like your customer. We can even talk about the employee experience and not just the customer experience.

The service-profit chain establishes relationships between profitability, customer satisfaction and employee satisfaction, loyalty, and productivity. The links in the chain are as follows: Profit and growth are stimulated primarily by customer satisfaction. Satisfaction is largely influenced by the value of services provided to customers. Value is created by satisfied, loyal, well-trained and productive employees. Employee satisfaction, in turn, results primarily from high-quality support services and policies that empower employees, which in turn inspires them to deliver results to customers.

Those insights have convinced ACI of the importance of assessing employee engagement considering their impact on the customer experience. Thus, in 2017 ACI World launched a new solution for airports, the Employee survey for Customer Experience (ECE). ECE is an internal diagnostic tool to assess the presence of the optimal conditions for a stronger commitment of airports' staff to customer experience, and can be deployed amongst the entire airport community, whether they work on the front line or back office. ACI's ECE program helps to create some synergy between employee experience and customer experience.

Great communication is vital in customer experience management. The way that you speak to your employees, customers, and colleagues generate emotions and help to create a strong engagement. Do not forget, the entire airport experience is all about emotions.

Dimitri Coll
Associate Director, Airport Service Quality (ASQ), Airports Council International - ACI World

Table of Contents

Introduction 1

Exceptionally Human Airports 7

Communication: Simple and Straight-Forward . . 23

The Big Three, Courtesy of Aristotle 45

How Credible Can You Be 61

Emotions Are The Message 79

Logically Speaking 99

Why Are We Doing This? Making
Exceptionally Human Communication
Work for Your Airport 121

Communication Skills Appendix 143

References 153

"Let's first establish the fact that caring is not a program, a technique, or something that can be taught or bought. It's not a quid pro quo, nor does it require you to coddle people, make them feel 'comfortable,' or provide false hope or security. Your team members are a lot more rational than they get credit for. They really don't expect a 'free ride.' They know that you can't insulate them from anxiety and job stress any more than their homeowner's policy can keep a hurricane from roaring through their neighborhood. They also know that you really can't guarantee their job security. But they do expect you to be fiercely committed to things like being scrupulously honest with them, believing in them, helping them succeed, and being there for them when they need it — and rightfully so. They know that when push comes to shove, you either care or you don't, and that nobody is a good enough actor to fake it for long."

—Bill Catlette and Richard Hadden,
Contented Cows Still Give Better Milk

Introduction

I've always loved airports. Even as a child, I felt a thrill when approaching an airport, driving on that stretch of road that demarks the everyday world from the world of flight. Growing up in Los Angeles, I had the good fortune to fly in and out of LAX, an elongated open-ended oval of terminals with a grand structure sitting in the middle of it all, what appears to be a flying saucer sitting on top of octopus-like tentacles that extend all the way to the ground. All this added to the sense of embarking on a fantastic voyage into the future.

Back in those days — the 70s and early 80s — security was more relaxed and any foreboding I had about flying was only in regard to the fear that we might fall out of the sky. The terminals at LAX were sleek and modern palaces where travelers passed the time before going through those magical portals that would take them to far-off destinations. I recall walking around the terminal looking at each gate and the posted destination city and being filled with wonder about each locale, working to find images to best match what each one looked like. New York. Honolulu. Phoenix. San Francisco. London. Philadelphia. Tokyo. Mexico

City. Chicago. Each city was added to an increasingly long list of places I wanted to see. Then we would arrive at our gate with our destination city posted, and the relationship between person and place got that much closer. Then the time would come for us to pass through those magic doors, head down the tunnel and right up to the plane where, with one final step, a new journey would begin — the journey of flight.

With eager eyes, I would look out the (usually PSA) airplane window and note all the tail markings on the planes from Asia, Latin America and Europe, not to mention all the domestic carriers such as PSA, Eastern, Western, Pan Am, Continental and TWA that now cease to exist. These tail emblems were chiseled into my young impressionable mind and upon arriving at our final destination and getting to our hotel, I would recreate the airport, making a dozen paper airplanes, each with the logo of one of the airlines, including even the iconic smile that was emblazoned on the nose of PSA planes. The "airport" was complete with gates that had small folded tent signs indicating which airline parked where, and I would move the planes around the invisible tarmac, preparing each for takeoff and eventual landing. It was a smooth affair, all positive, all joyous and all infectious, and I still find it a great thrill and a joy flying at this mid-century point in my life.

So, it should come as no surprise that I find myself

working with airports in their quest to create a stellar experience for all who pass through their doors, or shall I say, their TSA security checkpoints. Little did my childhood self know of the complexity and nearly impossible coordination that takes place within an airport's confines to create that experience. As it turns out, most people are not aware of how an airport operates. Most are unaware that an airport is an entity that directly employs a very small percentage of the workforce that make the place run or that each stakeholder, partner, governmental agency and airline have their own culture and approach to customer service, to what degree there is any customer service. People are also mostly unaware of the countless regulations airports must abide by or generally of how an airport actually works.

For some people, airports are more akin to a doctor's waiting room than they are to a desirable place to be. When thinking of those waiting rooms we've been in, it's not the waiting room that we ultimately came to visit, but rather the doctor who treats whatever condition we needed tending to. Those waiting rooms may be sparse and filled with magazines like People, Sports Illustrated, Time or Newsweek — nothing overtly political or emotionally charged, just publications to help pass the time. The lighting may be harsh and there may be background music. There may be some plants, framed posters of prints by Van Gogh or Picasso, as well as chairs that may or may not be comfortable. You may be waiting a few minutes or up to an hour, depending on the time of day and the popularity of the doctor. You may get annoyed, antsy or even angry because of the wait, but as soon as your name is called, all that falls to the wayside as you finally get to see that person you are there to see. If the doctor is that good or your malady such that he or she holds the most promise for bringing you back to good health, you'll tolerate practically any waiting room experience because there is little alternative.

Airports are transitional zones that on one level simply curate the time between passengers arriving and getting airborne. They are places that help pass the time, that hold our emotions in check so that we can eventually step onto an airplane that takes us to where we ultimately want to be. Airports are neither a place of departure nor of destination, rather they are facilitators of that experience, with the host city, state or country being that ultimate point in space. Airports are a "moment in time," not time itself.

At the same time, this "moment" has real world implications. Just as you might hesitate to see the same doctor again because you don't want to go through an unpleasant waiting room experience, we might hesitate to fly in to or out of a particular airport, assuming we

Introduction

actually have a choice, because the experience was that bad. But even if we don't have a choice, as most cities or regions are served by only one commercial airport, the impression that an airport makes upon us affects how we view that city or region, for better or worse, and the implications can be far reaching.

> *"Customer-driven service quality enhancements affect not only passengers' perceptions, but also the overall attractiveness of the airport relative to its competitors. Thus, allocating an appropriate amount of resources to the key factors of airport service quality can increase the likelihood of being perceived by a passenger as the best choice, relative to the alternatives available."*
>
> -Dale Fodness and Brian Murray

My ideal goal for this book is to help airport executives and all the people who work in airports recreate for their customers that thrill I felt as a child entering an airport. My more realistic goal is to help you create a more Exceptionally Human Airport Experience for your people, your partners at the airport and especially your customers.

An Exceptionally Human Airport productively engages its workforce. It is nimble and strategic with its communications. It uses the Three Pillars of Exceptionally Communication — trust, emotion and reason — to bridge divides internally and externally with its customers. An Exceptionally Human Airport can successfully connect with a variety of people in a variety of settings. Most of all, an Exceptionally Human Airport puts people first and communicates in such a way that everyone feels valued.

Chapter 1

Exceptionally Human Airports

"The most pressing challenge for an airport is to enhance the quality of the passenger experience."
– Brian Cotton

In his book, *The End of Airports*, Loyola University New Orleans Professor Christopher Schaberg explores the role airports play in modern society, making some keen observations about stresses related to air travel and taking sweeping jabs at airports themselves — namely, that airports simply do not care about people.

"At the airport no one cares about you; they just want your credit card; they just want to see you shuffle along and leave this space…at which point you will be acknowledged and thanked by hollow-eyed employees…."

For those of us who work within the airport space, this description borders on offensive. At the same time, Schaberg may be touching upon a sentiment shared by many travelers — the notion that airports do not care about people. Now, we know this is not true, but it's not necessarily our truth that matters, but rather the truth of the traveler and those who make up an airport's workforce.

I reached out to Schaberg and pointed out that there are teams of dedicated professionals who place significant personal, emotional, and financial resources into creating a better airport customer experience. Airports are concerned about their travelers and their workforce, very much so. His omission of this fact did airports a disservice. And to his credit, Schaberg thoughtfully replied. "I will readily admit that I have more questions than answers when it comes to airports."

In a 2007 article in Airport Management, respected airport expert Joanne Paternoster defined excellent customer service as, "the synergy created when an airport's ability to exceed its customer's needs and expectations consistently matches the customers' perception that their needs and expectations are well met." People bring their expectations and their emotional needs with them to the airport, and like it or not, airports bear the brunt of these expectations and emotional needs. The people who work within and around the airport will shoulder the responsibility of meeting these needs, whether they are

> *People bring their expectations and their emotional needs with them to the airport...*

aware of that fact or not, whether they like it or not, and whether they are properly prepared to play that role or not. Paternoster address this when she states, "effective and regular employee communications ensure that airport employees are the first to know about upcoming events, operational changes and capital construction, so that they not only feel that they are valued members of the airport family but they, in turn, can better anticipate customer needs, answer customer questions and participate in promoting the airport's image."

It is for these reasons that bringing "humanness" into our airports is critical for generating that Exceptionally Human Airport Experience. And the key to creating this experience is Exceptionally Human communication.

Air travel numbers over the past decade show a healthy and steady increase of travelers with predictions for that to continue well into the future, and all these travelers pass through our airports. Airports have responded to this increase by making their spaces more inviting, investing resources into making them more comfortable, and as much as possible, more relaxing. This effort has also included integrating advanced technologies which offer more ways to pass the time than just sitting in some uncomfortable chair next to a departure gate. All of these steps, and countless more, have had a positive impact.

At the same time, it still takes people to make an airport run. These people, these human beings, are still the primary source of experience creation for those who pass through the airport. Be it TSA, the airline ticket counter rep, the skycap or the person working the sunglasses stand, the interactions that take place between these folks and the traveler are the ones that leave a mark. These are the spaces that Vineet Nayar, former HCL Technologies CEO and author of the book *Employees First, Customers Second*, calls the **Value Zone**. Similar to what Dimitri Coll called touch points or moments of truth in the Forward, the Value Zone is the space in which an organization's employees and their clients, guests or customers interact. Nayar argues that these interactions are what ultimately shape the experience, beyond whatever product or service the organization offers. When you consider airports, there are countless Value Zone spaces, and often the employees filling these spaces are not direct airport employees themselves, but those of the numerous stakeholders and partners.

If the people occupying these critical spaces are lacking in the communication skills required to connect with the many travelers they interact with, then no matter how much an airport may invest in technology, redesigns, or even bathroom upgrades, the experience will remain sub par.

There are no more important skills to develop than human communication skills to help ensure a positive experience will happen. As Mark Drusch, Eliot Lees, and Stephen Freibrun note in their October 2017 Airport Business magazine article Reimagining the Passenger Experience, "The most successful airports and airlines will be those that can anticipate the diverse needs and desires of their travelers and create positive experiences for each of them."

Most people, from advanced degree holders to those who did not finish high school, have had precious few opportunities to develop their communication skill sets. This is why developing the Exceptionally Human communication skills of their people is a crucial step for airports to take, as these are the skills that are ultimately required to generate the traveler experience airports want to create.

> *"The most successful airports and airlines will be those that can anticipate the diverse needs and desires of their travelers and create positive experiences for each of them."*

As humans, we all have exceptional qualities. I use the words Exceptionally Human to highlight those aspects of our behavior that rise above and beyond the typical, usual or standard. Some of us are exceptional in mathematics or the sciences, some in athletics, and still others in the performing or visual arts. Some of us are exceptional spouses, parents, sisters, brothers, and friends. Growing up, I witnessed some Exceptionally Human communication, as my family had a hand in the Los Angeles entertainment industry. They were quite adept at verbally creating "realities". When I say that what I witnessed growing up was Exceptionally Human, I am referring specifically to a person's ability to master a complex set of skills so as to ensure that whatever it is they are communicating is paid attention to, and perhaps most importantly, listened to. Exceptionally Human communicators appear to effortlessly apply time-honored techniques, yet they do so in a highly strategic manner. Exceptionally Human communicators are able to recognize and understand what behaviors and words to employ and under what circumstances they are to be used. It may not be every time they communicate, but when the need arises, they are at the ready. And soon enough, that will be you as well.

> *Exceptionally Human communicators are able to recognize and understand what behaviors and words to employ and under what circumstances they are to be used.*

The best person to turn to for guidance as to how to become an Exceptionally Human communicator is the ancient Greek philosopher Aristotle. Aristotle was an exceptional human being. Perhaps his most significant and lasting achievement are his rhetorical proofs, the three essential items one must engage with to successfully attract and hold a person's attention. According to Aristotle, there is ***ethos***, the credibility you have and the trust you earn from people. Next, there is ***pathos***, the emotions you generate in others. And finally there is ***logos***, how reasonable people find your message based on the ideas, facts, and arguments you present. Trust, emotions, and reason are the three qualities Aristotle says we need to persuade people to take action, and the men and women who master these qualities enjoy extraordinary success. I like to refer to these as the Three Pillars of Exceptional Communication.

It is a tribute to the strength of Aristotle's insights that more than 2300 years after his death, trust, emotions, and reason are still the foundation of Exceptionally Human communication and the good results we hope to achieve from our interactions.

I think a lot about Aristotle's three elements. I think about them as a husband and the father of two young children. Marriage and children challenge your communication skills every day! I think about them professionally, as it's my company's job to help airports and other organizations, through their communication and interpersonal interactions, create exceptionally positive experiences for their people, their customers and their clients. More often than not, I think about these things most when I interact with businesses as a customer myself, when I'm at an airport or on an airline, or when I think back to those times when I was an employee.

Probably because one aspect of my work is focused on helping airports and other organizations create satisfying interactions with their clients and customers, I also tend to focus on whether these organizations create satisfying interactions with me. This is another way of saying I have high expectations. Or maybe what I really mean is I can be the guy who is a real pain in the butt. I try not to be that guy. But despite decades of yoga and daily t'ai chi practice as a means to ground myself, my moods still vary widely and so my reactions to businesses vary as well. Sometimes I am quite forgiving of oversights, missed appointments, defective products, and inattentive if not outright indifferent service. At other times my tolerance for these things sits at near zero and I almost instantaneously feel that surge of energy that comes right before an unpleasant outburst. I am not proud of myself when I lose my temper but I'm human. I have my good and bad days, and I don't like it when expectations fall short, when people fail to live up to their word or the promised deadlines are not met, especially as a customer or client.

Because I have a fair amount of experience being "that guy," I can tell you Aristotle's three elements, *ethos, pathos,* and *logos* — the Three Pillars of Exceptional Communication — have a huge influence on how I react. People who earn my trust, who I view as credible, who are aware of what feelings I might be experiencing, and offer a reasonable explanation, will not make me angry even when I am having the worst of days. These folks might tell me about a problem – about something that *should* make me angry – but it doesn't because the manner in which they have communicated exercised the best of what Aristotle's three elements offer. On the other hand, people who do little or none of the things Aristotle recommends can make me furious on the best of days. Even when the product or service involved in the transaction was suitable. I think of this as the meal-was-delicious-but-the-waiter-was-a-jerk problem.

Here's a good example of a person using the Three Pillars of Exceptional Communication. This post comes from our neighborhood's parent listserv:

We recently returned from our first family vacation, so some helpful info for those of you who may be traveling soon. We went through TSA at airport and got pulled aside because we had a jar of peanut butter in our carry on. TSA person said we couldn't take through. I told TSA we really needed the PB because it's one of a few things our kids reliably eat. TSA person noticed we had crackers in our carry on as well, and suggested that we go back out through security and make PB crackers, as we could take those through. He even got a plastic knife and plastic bag for us so we could make it hap-

pen. So helpful and understanding. We did that. Never did I think I'd be thrilled with TSA, but this guy was AMAZING.

Compare this to what another neighbor posted about a strikingly similar situation:

Family flyers beware! You cannot bring a plastic jar of peanut butter through security. Not knowing that, we had packed one in our carry on and TSA told us we could not. We lamented wasting the food aloud and the TSA woman shrugged her shoulders and sarcastically suggested we go outside security and eat the entire jar if we were that concerned. Of course we didn't do that, and she threw the PB out while telling us it was a shame we wasted that food. It's no wonder people hate the TSA.

Think about what the TSA agent created by taking an extra fifteen seconds to help my neighbor's family. He created trust and credibility and he created incredibly positive emotions. And he delivered the reasonable message that TSA really cares about people, not just about moving them through their security lines.

Trust, emotions and reason are so powerful that they can persuade us to become loyal customers of a company that has caused us a problem. They can also persuade us to never step foot again in a business that hasn't caused us a problem. According to Bruce Temkin, Managing Partner of Temkin Group, a customer service research and consulting firm, "When companies responded very poorly after a bad experience, 47 percent of consumers stopped spending completely with the company. When they had a very good response, only 6 percent stopped spending and 37 percent increased their spending… Consumers that are satisfied with customer service interactions are 4x's more likely to repurchase than those who are dissatisfied." So a good question to ask is what defines satisfaction, and my answer would be found in *trust, emotions and reason.*

The purpose of this book then is to help you use Aristotle's insights, the Three Pillars of Exceptional Communication, to more successfully communicate internally with colleagues and employees and with other stakeholders in your airport, as well as to help front line workers communicate more successfully with airport customers. To that end, I would like to say first that **you are already a good communicator.** We naturally communicate well with the spouses, partners, family, friends, co-workers and customers in our lives. Otherwise, we wouldn't have been able to develop relationships with them or remain gainfully employed. So the goal is not to get you to be a good communicator, but rather to help you become an Exceptionally Human communicator. I want you to become a Nobel Prize winning communicator, an undisputed National Champion communicator, a poster child for communication, or to put it quite simply, to become the best possible communicator a person can be. I want you to be *Excep-*

tionally Human!

Now, I feel it is important to say that this is probably, at the very least, an overly ambitious goal. My goodness, professional baseball players are considered highly successful when they *fail* to get a hit 7 out of 10 times, and in basketball missing 5 out of 10 shots is equally impressive. We are all human and that means we are all less than perfect, and will be less than perfect. Nobody will be the best communicator at all times, myself included. However, we can all continually get better and improve our chances of having more successful interactions, and as a result, more positive outcomes. Aim high! Aim higher than you might have previously imagined or thought possible, so that although you may not hit the mark every time, your overall performance will be that much more improved.

12 minutes in the morning, 12 minutes in the afternoon, that's all

In other words, I want to increase the probability that your communication will be outstanding. All I'm asking for is a modest and achievable 5 percent improvement, or focused effort, in your communication effectiveness. Five percent can be huge. Consider a 5 percent increase in customer satisfaction scores, a 5 percent increase in Net Promoter Scores or a 5 percent increase in ASQ scores or 5 percent increase in JD Power scores. As pointed out in Dimitri Coll's forward, a mere 1 percent increase in ASQ's global passenger satisfaction mean generates, on average, a growth of non-aeronautical revenue of 1.5 percent. One of our largest clients, Philadelphia International Airport, has a 14.4 billion dollar economic impact on the region. A percent increase on that front amounts to 720 million dollars. As I said, percent can be huge. At the same time, 5 percent is very achievable, in the same way taking 5 percent of the money you currently have in your wallet or purse and placing it into savings. It can most certainly be done. In a typical 40-hour workweek, 5 percent equals only 24 total minutes per day. A 5 percent focused effort, 12 minutes in the morning, and 12 minutes in the afternoon, can produce remarkable results, especially if that 5 percent is compounded, which it will be if you constantly strive for it. There is no end point, only continual and regular improvement, and with it, continual and regular results.

Let me tell you how I would like us to do this. First, I would like to talk about how communication actually works. I am going to dip into my graduate studies, but I promise this discussion won't be dry, academic or dull. There are fascinating insights from communication studies research that are simple to understand and have incredibly powerful possibilities when applied in our everyday work lives. This is the same material I use when teaching at the University of Pennsylvania's Organizational Dynamics program, so you too will get a dose of Ivy League education here.

You are going to hear me talk about two of these insights a lot. They are **perception** and **lack of control**. When we communicate, our message is what the other person perceives it to be and not necessarily what we intended. We all know how it feels to be misunderstood. We also lose control over our message the moment we speak it or send it. Then our message falls under the control of the person who receives it and sometimes we are really surprised by what they do with that message.

Next, we will talk about **communication competence** and our communication styles. What are our preferred modes of communicating with other people and what are the outcomes of those styles? We will also talk about adapting our communication style to the preferred style of the person receiving our message. Exceptionally Human communicators can spot the different communication styles of people and adapt their interactions from person to person, while still maintaining their integrity. This isn't always easy to do but when we do it right, the results can be phenomenal.

We will also take a more in-depth look at Aristotle's three rhetorical proofs, the Three Pillars of Exceptional

Communication: trust, emotions and reason. Yes, we're going to dip into some good old Greek philosophy, but in a fun, highly relevant manner. We are going to talk about how you can use these proven communications techniques to become more adept at the three elements, especially in an airport environment. These skills are most certainly acquirable, and although it does take some focused effort to harness the power in them, they can and will make an immediate and powerful difference in how well you communicate. We will break each element down and guide you toward mastering each one of them. Most importantly, we will provide some guidance as to where you can locate the places in your airport where having Exceptionally Human communication can make a real difference, places I like to refer to as **key organizational interactions**.

Throughout the book, we will talk about using different communication mediums, especially the newer electronic ones like email and social media. Digital communication tools are powerful, and airports are increasingly turning to them, but they come with special pitfalls. We will look at how to avoid the pitfalls and harness that power. Another change is the rise of "outstanding service" as the key value that differentiates one airport from another and especially an airport that receives higher satisfaction scores from an airport whose scores are less than where they want them to be.

We will finish up by reinforcing why *trust, emotions,* and *reason* are even more important to our professional success and the success of the airport we work at than ever before. They can teach you to become *Exceptionally Human* communicators and to thrive in today's world, approaching every interaction with integrity and having it received and perceived in the way in which you intended it. So, without further ado, let's head to the airport!

Chapter 2

Communication: Simple and Straight-Forward

"I found that when I wrote a very sad piece people were as apt to laugh as they were to be moved. So I gave up the notion of communication as impractical in my case."
–John Cage, Composer

    Here is something worth taking into serious consideration, however distressing it may be: You have precious little control of your communication. Hold on! How is that possible? In the last chapter, we agreed that all of us are pretty decent communicators, which means we *must* have some control over our messages, even after we send them, right? Well, sort of. There's an old axiom in the field of communication studies that says you cannot not communicate, that we are always communicating, whether we like it or not. That means that people are continually interpreting and ascribing meaning to our actions and behaviors, from what we say to what we wear. Consider the identification badge airport workers wear and the many interpretations travelers have of that badge: Information center, complaint center, reason for my plane being delayed or my baggage being lost. That leads into another axiom, which is once the message you are trying to communicate has left your body, be it written, verbal, or otherwise, you have in essence lost all control over its meaning. Control over the meaning of a message now belongs to the person or people you delivered it to. And their interpretation of the meaning may have very little to do with the actual intent of your message. People can ascribe meaning to just about anything you do or don't do, so the extent of control you have over your message is actually quite limited.

Think about the countless times in our personal and professional lives that we have carefully crafted the most accurate message possible, only to have the other person interpret it in a way that was quite different than what we intended. At an airport, it happens every day. The problem — this lack of control I refer to — comes from the place I call the **interpretive gap**. Interpretive gaps are those spaces between how we intend a message to be received and the meaning other people give to that message, the "filling in the blanks," so to speak. People interpret! People fill in the blanks! And more often than not, people fill in the blanks as they want to, or as they desire, not as we wish or hope they will. As much as airports work to create messaging and environments to cater to their workers' and their travelers' needs, it is ultimately the worker or traveler who will give meaning to the airport's efforts. As ACI's 2016 Passenger Personas demonstrate, there's a *"range of personalities, behaviors and needs"* for each traveler. Simply put, all our communication is at the mercy of those around us and we are dependent on their accurate interpretation in order to have quality communication. One of my goals is to help reduce the interpretive gaps between the people who work in and travel through airports, and as a result, increase the chances for understanding and a positively enhanced airport experience. To do this, let me talk briefly about what communication is and how it works. After that, I will reveal what we need to do to keep those interpretive gaps as narrow as possible.

What Communication Is (And Is Not)

When we think of communication, we may think about sending a text or email, talking on the phone, social media, and especially talking face to face. Communication is also something we absolutely take for granted; we think it is natural to take ideas and feelings that exist solely inside ourselves and communicate them in such a way that people understand them the same way that we do. We forget how truly remarkable our ability to communicate really is. How it works is remarkable too.

For simplicity's sake, let's say communication is something that occurs between two people: **the sender** and **the receiver**. The sender wants to take thoughts she has in her head, and/or feelings she has in her body, and express them so the receiver understands exactly what she is thinking and feeling. To do this, the sender must use **symbols**.

What are symbols? Definitively speaking, symbols are representations of something else. The words you are reading right now are symbols that represent thoughts and ideas. Facial expressions are symbols that represent how we are feeling. Think of the Stars and Stripes as being a symbolic representation of the United States, the red maple leaf as a symbolic representation of Canada, the tricolor of red, white and green as a symbolic representation of Mexico, or of any other nation's flag as being a symbolic representation of that nation. Symbols evoke thoughts and feelings in people who may or may not share a common understanding of what those symbols mean, but when they share the same meaning, they increase their chances of understanding each other. As humans, the most common symbol we use is language, and according to Ethnologue, an annual reference publication that provides information on languages of the world, there are over 7,000 actively used languages. It is through language that we attempt to communicate what we think and feel, and apparently we do so in 7,000 distinct ways!

Once our thoughts and feelings are symbolized, we have a **message**. This message is transmitted from the sender to the receiver through what is called the channel or medium. A medium can be verbal, it can be written and in the digital age, it can be visual by the posting of photos and videos. The **message** represents — and the key word here is *represents* — what the sender is thinking and feeling. Our hope is that the receiver interprets the message in such a way that understanding is achieved. It's a lofty goal and generally we do a surprisingly good job of it.

Yet, this rather simple way of looking at communication presents many challenges. The first of these challenges is **assumption**. The assumption is our expectation that the other person will interpret what we express in the way we intended, that the other person will know exactly what we mean when we make a statement or write an email or post a photo. The problem is that all symbols are subject to interpretation — those interpretive gaps, those "filling in of the blanks" we talked about earlier. With every symbol exchanged between people, the interpretive gap between what we intended to communicate and how it is received can become increasingly wide.

Sometimes that gap is quite large, such as when someone makes eye contact with you across a crowded room. Do they like you? Do they know you? Are they even looking at you? What are the many things that look could mean? Other times the gap is very narrow, such as when someone says, "You are a dear friend" in a sincere voice. But if said in a sarcastic voice, the gap opens wider. When an advertisement promises "the best in the world!" the interpretive gap can be so wide we couldn't see across it if we had binoculars. When we get a lawyer to review a contract that guarantees our satisfaction, there should be no gap at all.

In the end, it is the receiver who ultimately controls the meaning of our communication. This is another way of saying that our messages are what our receivers **perceive** them to be, and that perception is another key idea in communication that we really need to talk about.

> *In the end, it is the receiver who ultimately controls the meaning of our communication.*

To explain this idea further, let me tell you a story.

On The Jet Way

As some people may recall, the winter of 2015 was

Communication: Simple and Straight-Forward

a record setting, bone-chilling affair on the East Coast. For two days, I got a reprieve when I traveled to visit family back in Los Angeles where temperatures were in the low 60s. As I prepared to board my return flight back to Philadelphia, I stood in line on the jet way.

Given the 6:30am flight, like most flights nowadays, was completely full, people were required to check their carry-on roller bags. Standing at the lower end of the jet way were two baggage handlers who were preparing to take all the bags into the plane's belly. People were grumpy, not only because it was the early morning and they had to check their supposedly carry-on bags, but because they were leaving balmy Southern California and returning to the cold winter out east. It was snowing and sleeting back in Philadelphia on that March day. One of the baggage handlers, in a rather sarcastic and somewhat condescending tone, addressed the long line of people waiting to get on the plane.

"What in the world do all you people want to go back to Philadelphia for? Look at it outside here; it's a little cloudy but it's breaking up and the sun is coming out and it's nice and warm. I don't understand it."

Wait a second! Did this guy just say that? I'm originally from Los Angeles, and although I've adapted to winter, come March I much prefer warmth to cold. Not only that, I paid over $600 to make this trip on a crowded airplane and now I'm being taunted? What gives?

And it was pretty clear from the expression on the faces of everyone around me that his outburst was not appreciated.

As the line slowly marched forward, I wound up next to the guy. I asked him what he was thinking, having a little fun at the customers' expense. He said he was only kidding around by trying to inject a little humor, and the manner in which he expressed that to me led me to truly believe him. I mentioned what he said, and the way he said it, could easily be taken the wrong way given the circumstances — grumpy people getting ready to get on a packed plane heading toward freezing conditions. He concurred and we had a little laugh as I boarded the plane and he took the bags down below. I was fine as I'd had additional communication to close the interpretive gap, but who knows how other people felt. Perhaps they were pissed, perhaps they were offended or perhaps they didn't care, but all of them came to interpret the man's message in the way they *perceived* it, not necessarily the way he intended it. Oh my.

The Foundations of World Class Communication: Communication Competence in the Airport Environment

"Some travelers wish to experience the airport almost as a destination unto itself, with many options for leisure and entertainment, dining, fitness and shopping. Others want a more minimalist experience, moving as quickly as possible throughout the airport before and after their fights. Still others may need extra assistance to navigate through an airport. The challenge for the airport is to deliver the experience that each type of passenger wants, consistently and cost-effectively, despite the inherent complexity in meeting a wide variety of needs."

– *Rajiv Gupta and Vunnam Venkaiah*

So there are big challenges standing between us and our goal of becoming Exceptionally Human communicators. These challenges are lack of control, or interpretive gaps, and the receiver's perception. There are also communication challenges specific to front line workers in the airport environment.

The first of those is that the people in airports have spent hundreds of dollars just for the privilege of entering the facility — no ticket, no getting past the security checkpoint. Hence, all the passengers moving about an airport have made a significant financial investment to be there. In some cases this investment is relatively small in comparison to their overall income, but in other cases it is a very large investment indeed. Unfortunately, there is no way to know this by simply looking at them. In this case, you cannot judge a book by its cover.

The second attribute is that your typical passenger is stressed. For as much pleasure and enjoyment as travel can bring, it can also be a stressful experience. The potential for negative emotions to boil over is much higher at an airport than it is for most facilities.

> *The potential for negative emotions to boil over is much higher at an airport than it is for most facilities.*

The third attribute is that there is some uncertainty as to the outcome of a traveler's journey. Yes, they will arrive at their final destination eventually, but given the numerous factors that can impact travel, from weather to terror, there are some unknowns that have to be accounted for. By and large, uncertainty produces more negative feelings in people than it does positive ones, so ignoring this factor is unwise.

These challenges also directly impact the work of airport executives and managers because the challenges of people on the front lines are their challenges as well.

An important strategy for meeting these challenges and generating desired outcomes is becoming a competent communicator or having what is known as Brian Spitzberg and William Cupach's theory of **communication competence**.

Roughly defined, communication competence is when the manner — not the content — in which a message is communicated, is acceptable to both parties. Simply put, it's not what you say but how you say it that makes you a competent communicator. Being a competent communicator means you have the ability to craft and deliver your message in such a way that the person or people you are sending it to will find its crafting and delivery acceptable, even if they disagree with or find the content upsetting. Exceptionally Human communicators express themselves in a manner that is acceptable to both them and their receivers. It's really the ability to keep other people positively engaged with us.

The truth is communication competence takes a great deal of hard work and practice, as we are born communicators, but only very crude ones. As infants, we really only had one effective way in which we conveyed messages: crying. If we were hungry, tired, had a soggy diaper, or simply needed to be held, we cried. To those without children, all crying may seem alike. I can tell you from first-hand experience, it is not. After our oldest son was born, we found our apartment not only filled with new love and joy, but also plenty of crying. Over the course of those first weeks and months, my wife and I began to notice subtle variations in our son's crying that would inform us what he was trying to express. For instance, when he had short little bleating cries, he was hungry. When he cried with an extended whine, his diaper needed changing. But more often than not, we had absolutely no idea what he was trying to express when he cried. But at times, recognizing the distinctions between his various cries did help us give him what he needed and brought temporary peace to our home, however short-lived. At the same time, the rest of the world is not our parents, nor should it be, so this is only the beginning of our growth as communicators.

Fortunately, as we grow up we gain access to language and can begin to explicitly express our needs, and that's when we take the first steps to becoming competent communicators. At the same time, many of our fellow humans simply find crying out for their needs the best approach they have for getting them met. I think you know what I'm talking about here, but just in case you don't, let me put it more directly: some people will whaa whaa whaa their way through life, without any attempts whatsoever at becoming competent communicators. Bottom line, competence is a LEARNED behavior, one that requires practice, experimentation, failure, discipline and determination. The effort may seem rather significant, but the payoff is well worth the time invested.

What makes a competent communicator? It starts with recognizing there is no **one ideal way to communicate**. What works in one situation will not necessarily work in another. It may be perfectly acceptable to use sharp language and a direct manner with one person, but it may totally backfire with another. So, first and foremost, a competent communicator must **develop a large repertoire of communication styles**. That means for those of us who prefer using more direct and assertive communication approaches, we must begin to develop alternative approaches and vice versa. We must begin to take ourselves out of our communication comfort zones and start using methods, styles, and approaches that, although they may be initially uncomfortable, over time will produce positive outcomes

> *What works in one situation will not necessarily work in another.*

and become integrated into our overall communication efforts.

A classic difference between styles is the difference between East Coast and West Coast communication in the United States. As a person who grew up and went to college in Southern California, spent 20 years in San Francisco, had a couple short stints in New York City and now lives in Philadelphia, I can tell you the difference is real. On the East Coast, people tend to be more direct and in the cities, this directness can be accompanied with a hard tone. On the West Coast, people are less direct. They can be leisurely in getting to the point. One is not better than the other, they are simply different. For someone from the East Coast, West Coasters can seem rambling, aloof and wordy. For someone from the West Coast, East Coasters can seem blunt and rude. As I've spent more years on the East Coast, my communication has become more direct and to the point. So when I return to the West Coast, as I often do, my communication can take people aback, that is until I adjust and return to my West Coast ways. This adjusting is my attempt at being a competent communicator. And this adjustment is simple compared to the challenges faced by the front line workers in airports who can face a new communication style with each new person they talk to!

Second, where is this communication taking place? In other words, **what is the context**? Every place has its own implicit and explicit set of rules, and we want to clearly understand what those rules are to avoid any unintentional violations. Context is what grounds all communication and allows mutual meaning to be achieved. It is the frame around which communication is placed. If what is being communicated is done so absent of context, then all bets are off and achieving mutually satisfying communication is left to chance. People often behave differently in their hometowns where they know they may meet a person again, as opposed to out of town, where they know they probably won't see the same person in the future. Context rules, figuratively and literally, and we must know the rules to know what is acceptable and what is not. In airports, this is especially true.

Finally, consideration must be given to the following two questions: **What is our goal?** And **what is our relationship with the other person?** For instance, if we have a dispute we wish to resolve with a neighbor, we may take a more congenial communication approach to resolve the matter, as this person lives next to us and as a result, we want to keep things on good terms. However, if our dispute is with a person at a company in another state or country that we don't intend to do business with again, we may be more direct or aggressive, as our relationship with them is far more distant and the chances we'll need something from them in the future are rather limited. This is a frequent challenge in traveler communications at airports, as in many cases the interactions people have are perceived to be one-time affairs, not long-lasting relationships. Although within the airport community itself the reality is quite the opposite, as these working relationships are of a more long-lasting nature.

Empathy also plays a key role in competent communication. Feeling what another person is feeling, or attempting to understand how they might feel, will help inform our communication choices. If I anticipate the person may get upset with the information being delivered, I may try to deliver it in such a way that at least doesn't intensify the negative feelings. Think back to the two TSA-peanut butter stories as a salient example. Empathy goes a long way toward avoiding unnecessary messiness in communication, because if you can anticipate how a receiver may emotionally respond to you, you can make choices that bring about a more desirable emotional response.

Here's a good personal example that, although not airport-based, illustrates this point very well. One recent night, my wife and I had one of our coveted date nights. The kids were with their grandparents and we had a night to ourselves. We decided to see a film and centered our evening around the screening time. We planned to have a relaxing dinner prior, but as we kicked back in our temporarily responsibility-less, child free home, we lost track of time and suddenly the starting time of the movie was closing in. Because of this, a relaxing sit-down dinner became impossible, so we grabbed a quick bite, hurriedly ate, then hailed a cab to the movie theater. Upon arriving at the theater, utility trucks were everywhere and two people in beach chairs were camped in front of the entrance. We were informed that the theater was closed due to an underground utility fire that had left several blocks without power for two days.

As you might imagine, we weren't thrilled. The theater website had no notice of the closing and had we known ahead of time, we would have planned things differently. But, such is life. And as you also might imagine, the two workers informing theatergoers of the closing weren't thrilled either, having to repeat the same story to countless disappointed people for the past two days. This was hardly a win-win situation.

I asked the theater employees why the information wasn't on the website. My question was met with a shrug. We were told we could go to another theater close by that would be showing the same film an hour and a half later. When we pointed out that would be too late for us, one of them said, "Bummer." Bummer? Bummer! We walked away not only disappointed, but a little pissed off as well.

Yes, bummer indeed. Bummer for us, as we infrequently have a night to ourselves and we scheduled this one around something that wasn't even going to happen. Bummer for those guys who had to deal with disappointed person after person. And bummer for the businesses who were losing out on profits because of something outside of their control — bummers all around.

Think about how my wife and I would have felt if instead of being disappointed on one of our rare date nights, we were taking a quick two-day vacation by ourselves and our flight was delayed for several hours. That would be a much bigger bummer and we might be even more pissed off, even though we both understand delays happen and the person telling us about the delay is not responsible for causing it. All the same, saying "bummer" to us in this case is definitely not a good idea! It was like saying "Too bad" or "That's life." Now, those things may be true, but they don't help the situation, they exacerbate it. Such a response doesn't make someone want to do business with that entity again. Common sense would dictate not saying "bummer" in a situation such as this, but we know from experience "common sense" is less common than we might hope for, hence this book.

A better way for airports to communicate is to acknowledge a person's inconvenience or hassle and to express empathy for their disappointment. Doing so won't resolve the situation, but neither will it create an opportunity for someone to take his or her frustration and disappointment out on you and your airport. That really would be a bummer. In fact, expressing empathy can lead to increased customer loyalty. That's an Exceptionally Human insight and at the same time it often takes some professional development for many people to know how and when to express empathy.

Achieving competence requires repeated practice and effort, while keeping in mind mistakes will be made. But it is worth it in the long run, as it will allow you to create greater and more meaningful connections with a wider range of people. For anyone learning how to play chess, one of the first lessons is to look a few moves ahead before moving. Communication researchers Brant Burleson and Scott Caplan refer to this quality as **cognitive complexity**. And in our communication practices, this generally means consciously recognizing what potential consequences are associated with our communication choices. In working to understand the possible outcomes to our communication style, we will better inform ourselves as to what is necessary to become a competent communicator. It does require us to go outside of our comfort zone, to try something new, to face failure. We will not get it right every time, but over time, we'll get it right more often than not, and that can make a huge difference. As one of my t'ai chi instructors likes to playfully say, "You'll never be perfect at t'ai chi, but with regular practice, your t'ai chi will be a little less wrong each time."

It is easy to think of many examples where being a competent communicator would have made our lives better. We have all had arguments with spouses, partners, family members, friends or business colleagues that we regret. Most of the time, we probably don't regret that we addressed the issue at the heart of the argument; we just don't like that we argued about it. We wish we had been kinder, more patient, more understanding and more respectful. We wish we could have expressed ourselves in a different way and had listened better, as well as been listened to better. We wish we had been able to discuss the issue without arguing. It is human for people to disagree, especially when they are disagreeing on things that are important to them or when they are under stress in places such as airports. Competent communicators can disagree with people and still make them feel good, and that's what being Exceptionally Human is all about.

Disagreements happen all the time, especially in the fast-paced and unpredictable airport environment. In fact, disagreements and conflict are built into the heart, bones and muscles of being human. I firmly believe, however — and I know I'm not alone — that success in business and at airports comes from good relationships more than anything else. Exceptionally Human communicators are superb at negotiating, proposing, selling, persuading and disagreeing with a wide range of people while still maintaining relationships with them. To this end, there are a lot of practical communication techniques that, although they take effort, are easy to learn and use, and can help your airport become that undisputed National Champion, Exceptionally Human Airport. And that takes us right back to our good friend, Aristotle.

> *Exceptionally Human communicators are superb at negotiating, proposing, selling, persuading and disagreeing with a wide range of people while still maintaining relationships with them.*

Chapter 3

The Big Three, Courtesy of Aristotle

"I know of only two other figures besides Aristotle who are equally revered in Western and Islamic traditions; Moses and Jesus. Now that tells you something about the company Aristotle keeps."
–Anonymous

If you take the time to consider the people who have most influenced you, inside an airport or otherwise, a few things should come to mind. First, they are typically people you perceive as credible and who you trust. Second, they are probably people who, when you think of them, elicit more positive emotions than negative ones. In other words, you generally feel good when they come to mind. Finally, when they are communicating with you, you'll more often than not perceive their communication to be reasonable and rational. Trust, emotions and reason is the remarkable combination of attributes that will keep people engaged with you, or if perceived negatively, will push them away. Once again, Exceptionally Human communication boils down to how trust, emotions and reason are perceived, and this is where Aristotle returns to center stage.

Most people are familiar with Aristotle, if not well, then by name at least. As a little refresher, Aristotle was an ancient Greek (from Macedonia) philosopher who wielded great influence not only in Greece, but also across the world. He is one of the few human figures equally revered in both Western and Islamic traditions. In addition to being a philosopher, Aristotle was a biologist, physician and overall human wonder. He had an amazing ability to remain in uncertain or highly ambiguous situations for prolonged periods of time without giving in to the burning desire to form a logical or reasonable explanation as to what was unfolding around him. This negative capability, as the poet John Keats termed it, is what allowed Aristotle to be such an amazing and insightful observer of animal behavior. In his capacity as a biologist, he made detailed discoveries about animals that in some cases were not confirmed by science until several centuries later. And it is because of this ability to observe and understand feral animal behavior that when he turned his attention to another animal's behavior — humans — his observations and conclusions were equally remarkable and are as relevant today as they were 23 centuries ago.

The Big Three, Courtesy of Aristotle

Aristotle observed that for one human to persuade another human, three things are required. Roughly translated, Aristotle discovered what I like to refer to as the instinctual cues we need to provide fellow human beings so they will strongly consider what we request of them. These three essentials are known as Aristotle's Rhetorical Proofs, and as mentioned in the introduction, they are *ethos*, *pathos*, and *logos* — or trust, feeling and reason. *Ethos* refers to your credibility or how much trust you have earned in others. *Pathos* refers to the emotional response or feelings generated in the person with whom you are communicating. Finally, *logos* refers to how reasonable, rational and logical the other person finds your position, request or argument to be. *Ethos*, *pathos* and *logos* are amongst the most significant and powerful insights into human behavior that have ever been made. The person able to master these three elements can essentially get people to do as they would like them to do, in an almost instinctual animal-like way. Now that's power.

I bring Aristotle's Rhetorical Proofs to your attention because first and foremost, they are Exceptionally Human. As you might imagine, this power has been used for better and for worse throughout human history. Our goal, of course, is to use this power to better our communication practices, so it's essential to keep in mind that these three essentials are fluid at all times and under all conditions. Credibility can take years to earn and only seconds to lose, and just because we've established initial credibility does not mean we will remain credible over time. In an airport, the time allowed to establish credibility is much less than the time it takes to lose it. The same holds true for emotions and logic, as feelings are fleeting, and logic applied to one situation will not necessarily translate to another setting. If the logic we provide is suspect, our credibility can suffer, or if your communication causes someone to feel anxious or nervous, then your logic may not be seen as sound. In other words, Aristotle's Rhetorical Proofs don't exist in separate compartments; they are interrelated, interconnected and utterly dependent on each other. So let's take some time now to fully grasp the significance of Aristotle's insights so your airport's communication can become that much more Exceptionally Human.

> *Credibility can take years to earn and only seconds to lose...*

This is my please-don't-try-to-understand-us story: My wife and I had recently hired a designer to assist us with a home project. The designer initially met with us and thoughtfully asked us questions as to why we wanted what we wanted and what we hoped the final result would look and feel like. We were uplifted and highly optimistic after this initial meeting; the designer seemed genuinely interested in meeting our needs. When the initial plans arrived, we were surprised to discover what we outlined in the meeting was only minimally present in the plans. When we spoke to the designer about this, we were told to simply use them as a starting point, provide our feedback, and then modifications would be made to best address our needs. So we did.

When the second round of plans arrived, we were dumbstruck. In spite of our direct feedback, these plans incorporated none of it — at all. We felt frustrated and disappointed. In a thoughtful and carefully crafted email, we expressed our unhappiness with these revised plans, and how our expressed needs were not being taken into consideration. We felt as if we were not being listened to, and how the designer responded to the email only reinforced our experience.

She responded, "Sorry to hear of your frustration. We work hard to ensure our clients are satisfied with the work done. We have put thoughtful work into this project. We would be happy to explain to you the reason and rationale behind our efforts, so you can better understand why we did what we did. We have some time later this week." In other words, she was asking us to understand them better, not to understand us better. Whoa! Wait a minute! What's going on here? Not once did the designer express any desire in writing to understand why we were feeling frustrated. Not once did she express any desire to want to know more about how we felt our needs weren't being taken into consideration. Instead, we simply received an offer to hear them out, to better understand them. Huh?

Let's take into account this designer is well respected, had ample glowing references, and clearly had great confidence in the work she did. She probably isn't accustomed to receiving negative feedback from her clients. As often happens in situations like this, the expert will exert their credentials and expertise as a way to bring about understanding. This may be fine for brain surgery, but can backfire elsewhere. And in this case, after multiple interactions where we felt our feedback wasn't taken into account, it did. We ceased our working relationship with this designer and sought assistance elsewhere. Had she only inquired as to why we were frustrated and taken the time to really listen to what we were saying, we may have continued the relationship. But she didn't. Instead, she asked us to understand them, not the other way around. More often than not, this will undermine credibility and prematurely end what could have been a positive working relationship.

I believe the airport executives and managers reading this book will find a lot of familiar ideas and feelings in this story. Consider the traveler seeking understanding who receives a "see it our way" response as opposed to a "we do see it your way" response. It is also important to the morale of your front line workers that their feelings are heard and valued, especially when often you can't change the challenges of their work environment. And positive working relationships with your colleagues and stakeholders in the other organizations that help the airport operate smoothly are absolutely essential because, while my wife and I could fire our designer, you often cannot fire your partners in the airport, and you most certainly cannot fire your travelers. You have to work well with them. And good communication is essential to doing that!

Ethos (Trust)

Consider the people you trust and find credible. Now compare them to people you distrust or find deceptive. The difference between the two groups is huge, is it not? So, gaining another person's trust and being seen as credible in their eyes should be of paramount importance. It is, in fact, essential. And when we are talking about our communication practices, it is important to recognize what it is specifically about our communication that builds trust and establishes credibility. To that point — and this is crucial to remember — no relationship, business, personal or otherwise, will remain intact if trust and credibility are absent.

And here's another important point: You are only as credible and trustworthy as other people perceive you to be credible and trustworthy. It does not matter how you think of yourself, but what others think of you that matters. The elements that will help elevate or diminish your credibility and trust is as much a matter of *how* you communicate as it is *what* you communicate. Actions do speak louder than words, and more often than not the *how* will outweigh the *what* of your message. Your tone, your speech rate, the words you choose and the medium through which you communicate will greatly influence the level of credibility and trust others have in you. For better or for worse, credibility also comes from your appearance, from your education and experience, and from what customers, and colleagues say about you. Credibility also comes from your online presence such as websites and social media accounts.

Trust is a bit more slippery to establish. I firmly believe we earn it by making others understand we think they are important to us. One way to do this is to demonstrate that we are committed to really listening to them and understanding what they want and need, that we are focused on them and not on ourselves. Another way we build trust is to show we value people.

> *Another way we build trust is to show we value people.*

The Big Three, Courtesy of Aristotle

Let me tell you a quick story about David L. Cohen, Senior Executive Vice President of Philadelphia-based Comcast Corporation. Cohen is a very busy person, to say the least, but I had the opportunity to meet him at a local business function where he was speaking. During our brief conversation we exchanged business cards. The following day, I sent a short email to him, thanking him for his presentation and the commitment Comcast has made to the City of Philadelphia. I didn't really expect a reply, but I was hoping he might remember me. Within the day, Cohen replied back. This is a man who is the number two executive at Comcast, one of the largest and most powerful companies in the United States. A man who has sat down before more Senators, members of Congress and Presidents than most of us combined ever will. And who was I? Compared to Comcast, I was smaller than small. Yet, he replied. Whether it was him or his executive assistant really doesn't matter. I received a reply! Cohen is clearly committed to making everyone he meets feel valued, and that boosts his credibility. And when you look at his success, you can see that it works! We'll talk about *ethos* more in Chapter 4.

Pathos (Emotions)

You know that saying, the one that goes, "People

may not remember your name, the company you worked for, or even where they met you, but they will remember how you made them feel." Well, in some ways that is *pathos*. Simply put, *pathos* is eliciting a desired emotional state in another person. When Aristotle wrote about *pathos*, he was tapping into a key element of persuasion; the idea that the emotional state of others significantly impacts their ability and willingness to listen to us. In other words, if we overlook how our communication alters another person's emotional state, we quite possibly are negating our entire communication effort. Think about it. When we are in a good mood, we are probably more willing to listen to information we don't necessarily agree with as compared to when we are in a bad mood or stressed out. Or, as Aristotle says in Lane Cooper's seminal 1932 book *The Rhetoric of Aristotle*, "…we give very different decisions under the sway of pain or joy, and liking or hatred."

> ...the emotional state of others significantly impacts their ability and willingness to listen to us.

Once again, and it can't be said enough, *pathos* is about other people's emotions. The emotions we express certainly count, but most important are the emotions we unleash in others, and that is often not in our control. And to truly understand the impact of that, it demands that we employ empathy. Empathy is one part the ability to understand, and I might add respect, what other people are feeling. More importantly, empathy is the ability to put ourselves in another person's emotional shoes to feel what the other person is feeling. Too often we forget the immense power emotions have on people and the power our communication has to impact the moods of others, especially at an airport. A simple smile or hello can go a long way towards building good relationships. A short quip to a question, or an unreturned smile can have the unintended consequence of eliciting a negative emotional reaction whose origin will be directly traced back to us. Ultimately, this could erode our credibility and/or limit the receptivity others have to our message. More often than not, we want the opposite of that.

Let me tell you a little story that made a big difference. When we were living in San Francisco, my wife and I were traveling with our first son to meet much of her East Coast family for the first time. It was a long flight. We were tired, our son was definitely tired (we could tell because he was screaming), and all the luggage from the flight had appeared except our car seat, which we absolutely needed. The woman at the airline baggage customer service counter could have just taken our name, given us a loaner and sent us on our way. Instead, she made three calls, sent someone to look for the seat, and actually found it for us. She told us, "I have young kids too." To this day, when I think about the airline she worked for and the airport we were at, I remember her and smile.

Logos (Reason)

Roughly speaking, *logos* refers to the use of reason or logic. Reason and rationality are what distinguish us from all the other species on our planet. Our beautiful cerebral cortex is what gives us the ability to make logical arguments as a means to persuade others or get others to see our point of view. It is a truly powerful tool we use every day, often without giving it a second thought. And what's so intriguing about *logos* is that what may seem logical and reasonable under one set of circumstances may not in another and vice versa. Airports are a perfect example of that, as what is reasonable there and what the rules and regulations are about what can and cannot occur there, can be much different than those outside the airport property.

Aristotle spoke to the power of *logos* when suggesting that the logic or reason presented does not necessarily need to be true, but only true to those who are receiving it, or more importantly, how they perceive it. And again, it's not always in our control. In fact, there are many instances when improper logic is viewed as both reasonable and rational when it is not. That is to say, under the right conditions, a completely illogical position, or what are academically referred to as fallacies, can appear logical, so long as *ethos* and *pathos* are in their proper place. Also, bear in mind, what may seem reasonable and rational to us may not be so for other people. Therefore, it is always important to ask ourselves the questions: Does this seem reasonable to them? Is the information we are presenting clear, accurate and relevant? Does it contain the information they need and want to know? This is not necessarily the same as telling them everything there is to know about the topic.

A good example of applied *logos* took place during a family trip to New York City when I took our young sons, Asa and Levi, to ride the subway train. They are both full-fledged public transit enthusiasts. When we got to the ticket machine, a man claiming he had a $10 ticket that he would sell to us for only $5 approached us. Being a veteran city dweller, I've seen this play before, so I told him we were only buying a $3 ticket and that his proposition wouldn't work for us. Applying additional logic, he persisted, saying for an extra $2 we could have $10 worth of rides. Again, I told him we only needed a $3 ticket. He continued to tell us how for an extra $2 we would have $7 additional dollars in rides. He then put the ticket into the vending machine to verify there was indeed $10 on it and continued to tell me what a great deal this was. He looked at Asa and Levi and mentioned how many more rides my sons would be able to take now that his daddy had an additional $7 in fare. It was true, the boys loved riding the subway, and we would actually need to ride it a couple more times. I relented, handed the man $5, and as if to reinforce his sincere logic, walked us right to the fare gate and made sure the ticket actually worked, and indeed it did. *Ethos*, the first proof, may not have been initially present, and *pathos*, the second proof, was not exactly working for him, but his *logos*, the third proof, was quite clear and ultimately overshadowed the other two. Ironically, the ticket stopped working after that initial ride, so eventually logos was lost as well, but we did get to where we needed to go, so it worked well enough. We'll talk about *logos* more in Chapter 6.

Communication competence and Aristotle's three elements walk hand in hand. Some people have a high demand for ethos from people. These men and women are the people in the world who say, "Prove to me you are credible and earn my trust. Then don't bother me with the details. Just go do the job!" On the other hand, some people want to know every detail of everything every step along the way. They are *logos* heavy. It is not that we haven't earned the trust of people like this, it is just that they want to know all the information as well. Same holds true for travelers, be it business or leisure, as well as airport partners and stakeholder employees. From the following examples, we can begin to see what our preferred or default communication styles are: How do we like to communicate? Do we like to be direct and get to the point? Or do we like to get to know a person before we get down to brass tacks? Do we want just the key points or the whole picture? Does a highly confident person impress us or does too much confidence make us suspicious? How much confidence do we express when we talk?

We instinctively respond to someone who has the same communication style we do. Most of us don't do it consciously, we just know we like the person and say, "They speak my language." We also feel, almost instantaneously, when a person has a vastly different style and that can have the opposite effect. Give a person who just wants to know what they need to do all the details as to why they need to do it and you will bore and frustrate the hell out of her. Give a detail-oriented person just the highlights and he will huff "You didn't answer my questions." A person who loves empathy will be hurt and offended if you look at him and say, "Yeah, I can fix that. Just give me a minute." And a person who just wants you to fix a problem does not want to spend ten minutes listening to a story about how one time you had the exact same problem, and oh how difficult it was.

None of these communication styles is right or wrong. They are just our personal styles — our Exceptionally Human styles. You can see from these examples why Exceptionally Human communicators adapt their communication styles to those they are communicating with. Adapting our communication style to the style of another person isn't about manipulating or lying to them. It isn't about tricking or fooling them. We aren't playing mind games. And we aren't selling ourselves out in any way. What we are doing is simply making the wants and needs of the other person in the interaction more important than our own, and in this time where travelers can feel less than important, this is key. We are showing we understand them and value them enough to make that effort. When we do, we increase the likelihood they will feel positive about the interaction and that it will be a successful one. And how they experience and perceive your airport will be positive as well. What we are doing is being a competent communicator through the application of Aristotle's three elements. What we are being is Exceptionally Human!

Chapter 4

How Credible Can You Be

"Trust is the currency of interactions."
-Rachel Botsman, Who Can You Trust?

What is credibility and how do we build it? Aristotle said that credibility can come from the manner and style in which we present ourselves. If we act credibly and trustworthily, it increases the chances that we will be perceived as credible and trustworthy. Aristotle also stressed the importance of "probity," which means we have strong moral principles, honesty and decency. Today, we would probably use a word like integrity to describe these qualities. If we are seen as having integrity, our credibility rises. On the other hand, if we are seen as lacking integrity, our credibility falls, and hopefully it doesn't crash completely.

In today's world, we know that the general public tends to have a less-than-desired perception of airlines and, consequently, airports. Crowded planes, security hassles, delays and general stress are multiple opportunities to enhance your airport's credibility. Integrity extends specifically to how quickly we reply to other people and how much we focus on their needs compared to our own. Our actions as well as our words build our credibility. Our credibility is also impacted by how people perceive we feel about them, which may or may not be how we meant them to feel, or even about how we actually feel about them.

In this chapter we'll explore ways we can increase our credibility in an airport setting and build trust in the process. It is essential to keep in mind that if we don't earn credibility and build trust in the hearts and minds of the people who work in and travel through our airports, the chances are good that anything we say to them will fall on deaf ears. We will focus on two areas of credibility. The first is response time. The second is focus.

If You Care You Will Answer RIGHT NOW

One measure that distinguishes world-class athletes from the weekend warrior is a highly developed response reflex. Professional athletes will respond to events and circumstances around them in impressively short time periods, whether hitting a ball or stopping a puck, those fractions of a second can be the difference between victory and defeat. The same principle can be applied to our communication with others. It is easy for those of us who grew up before the internet era to be puzzled by the fact people have an expectation for an immediate reply today. However, the "right now" expectation is real and has real implications.

Chances are, you have countless interactions at your airport. Be it with front-line personnel, landside operations, travelers, the TSA or airport executives, you have your own criteria for determining who deserves your full and immediate attention.

Let's use this digital example: When you send a work-related email to someone, how quickly do you expect a reply? And if you don't receive a reply as quickly as you expect or desire, how do you start to feel about the other person? In your mind, what happens to their credibility, their trust and their reliability? My guess is that it takes a little ding or experiences a slight diminishment. Contrast that with what happens when you receive a reply within the time period you expect. What then happens to their credibility, their trust and their reliability? It's probably safe to say it goes up, or at the very least, remains where it was prior to you receiving the reply.

So, what are the criteria you use to determine who gets your full attention first? Is it the content, or the subject matter? Is it the person or how important you determine that person to be? My guess is that it's all of the above, if not some combination. But how urgently they want your attention is a good place to start. If you begin by first and foremost thinking about the other person, then it's much more likely that you'll meet their expectations because after all, you are thinking about them first. And in doing so, you both consciously and unconsciously send that person a message that their expectations truly matter, and that will naturally increase your credibility in their eyes. The name of the game here is to build credibility and trust and by them perceiving that their needs matter, you do just that.

When you give others 100% of your attention, they will be more likely to support you the next time you need their assistance or input. This is an important factor when attempting to generate buy-in and commitment from your airport's workforce. Focus on the other person first. If we put the wants and needs of the other person first, and if an airport's workers sense that their needs are prioritized, then the chances of creating an exceptionally positive outcome increase. There are four ways I'd like to discuss that do this: Make the other person feel important, recognize stress, try to see the balance between the understanding and solutions the person wants, and use the word "you" instead of the word "I."

Feeling Important

Most people like to feel important. Some people expect it. Sometimes it is earned, other times it's not. Just consider the investments airlines make in the front-of-the-plane experience compared to the back of the plane. Some travelers may have a burning desire to feel important, yet they will not or cannot express their desire. In our communication with others, we may communicate in a manner that makes them feel important and at other times we may communicate in a way that makes them feel they are not. The same can be said of the airport workforce. Some may be there for solely financial reasons, while others feel deeply invested in the airport experience. What's tricky here is knowing: first, if the other person wants to feel important and second, if our communication is indeed expressing that sense of importance. In many ways it comes down to focus. When we place our focus on another person, we are saying to them that they are important, that what they have to say is important and that what they are feeling is important.

In some cases, it's quite clear who wants to feel important. People who have high status and rank can be amongst those. A title or credential can help tell us if someone is important, who has access to an airline lounge or has "priority" printed on her boarding pass.

At the same time, I don't know too many people who like to feel unimportant. As a matter of fact, when we communicate in a manner that tells the other person they are important, and they don't necessarily expect that, our credibility will go that much higher as a result. Consider the front-line airport employee who receives unexpected praise from the airports CEO. We are defying their expectation in a positive way. When we make everyone feel important, we build credibility across the board, regardless of status, power or position. So, consider making everyone feel important, not just those who we believe to be important. This may be difficult at an airport where status and rank are often prized commodities; nonetheless, the benefits are worth the effort. We never know when we will need to work collaboratively with others in the future or what travelers may go home and speak highly of your airport to potential future visitors. Making everyone feel important builds credibility and trust.

> *So, consider making everyone feel important, not just those who we believe to be important.*

How do you help people feel important? Make sure the conversation is focused on them and reply in a timely manner. Doing these two simple things will go a long way to boost your credibility in their eyes. It doesn't take much to make people feel important. Consider this story:

I was having lunch at a Mexican restaurant in an airport on one of my recent trips. Every seat was taken and folks were standing around both waiting to order and waiting for their orders. From my counter seat, I watched the cooks cranking food out; all eight burners were sizzling up tacos, burritos and grilled meats. The manager was scrambling, putting hot dishes on the service trays along with a side of chips and either a small cup of guacamole or salsa. He then called out order numbers so customers could claim their prize. It was a smooth operation.

After the owner called out number 74, a customer walked up, retrieved her food and just before walking away, paused. She glanced down and up and down again. The manager turned away to prepare another tray when the customer inquired, "Can I have the guacamole instead of the salsa?" The manager turned back to her and then looked down at the guacamole container that lay empty on the counter. He then started to say, "Sorry, we're out of…" then stopped. He then momentarily ducked behind the kitchen wall, emerging with a small to-go container with guacamole in it, and handed it to his customer and said, "You're welcome to have both." It all took less than ten seconds. She was happy.

Less than ten seconds. The manager could have easily completed his sentence, "Sorry, we're out of guacamole," and moved on. It probably would not have been a big deal. It would certainly be understandable, given how busy it was, for items to run out. I'm sure she would have understood and thought nothing of it. But that's not what happened. He made a split second decision that then took less than 10 seconds to execute, and for that, she did think something of it. She said thank you, he smiled and I think it's safe to say that if that woman is a frequent traveler and comes through that airport a lot, she'll come back to the same restaurant and have good things to say about that airport.

See Stress in Other People – Help Them Reduce It

We live in a stressful world. We all experience stress. Airports are stress hotbeds! None of us enjoy it. And many of us do not think or act our best when we are under stress. It causes us to enter into a fight or flight response. We either increase our efforts or we withdraw from the situation. At work, this can translate into trying to work harder and harder, perhaps even becoming somewhat of a "bull in a china shop" character. Or we might retreat into our own inner world and shut others out. I know that when I'm under stress, I tend to fall into the "fight" category and my actions and behavior can come across as aggressive, terse and blunt. Very rarely will I actually tell people that I'm under stress. Who likes to admit it?

An Exceptionally Human part of stress is that it affects how we behave in situations, regardless of whether those situations are the cause of the stress or not. For example, before a big business trip, I can be very keyed up. I'm feeling the positive stress that — at the right level — gives me energy and focus. But in this state, there have been times I have wanted to yell "Come on, let's go!" when the line at the airport, regardless of what line it is, *feels* like it is moving slowly. The person serving at the ticket counter, security checkpoint or concession stand isn't causing my stress. It has nothing to do with her. But if she smiles and says "Sorry for the wait," then their credibility rises with me. I walk away feeling good about her, better about myself and more satisfied with our very simple exchange. It very much transforms my experience.

As we've already discussed, airports are environments in which a very large portion of customers are under stress. Travel itself is stressful, particularly for the occasional traveler, when delays, missed connections, lost luggage, weariness and hunger can all place a strain on people. Business travelers are often keyed up like me before a big presentation because most of them only travel when the business is important enough to justify the time and cost of the trip. And then there is a third factor that causes stress — people who are not stressed are surrounded by people who are, and soon the unstressed people begin to feel stressed as well. And this dynamic affects both travelers *and* people who work in airports.

One intriguing quality about being human is that we have the ability to catch things from one another. We know that if we are around somebody who is sick with a cold or the flu, we might get sick ourselves. What's not so widely understood is that we can also catch each other's emotions. This is called Emotional Contagion. We can catch each other's emotions at home, at play and at work. Have you ever noticed that when you spend time around negative people, you find yourself beginning to feel negative as well? The same can be said about being around positive people. If you spend time around positive people you too will begin to feel more positive. Sigal Barsade, Ph.D., in a Psychology Today article, wrote, "Research reveals that emotions, both positive and negative, actually spread … like viruses." People routinely *catch* each other's feelings when they are together in groups whether those groups are at home, at school, in the neighborhood, at work and especially at the airport. Consider the JFK or LAX mass

> *We can catch each other's emotions at home, at play and at work.*

panic incidents that occurred in 2016 and you'll recognize how quickly emotions can spread amongst people.

Be it hurricanes, terror, overbooked flights or lost luggage, airports are emotionally charged spaces. First, there are the travelers who are often stressed, worried and anxious. Next, there are the airport employees who may or may not in the best mood themselves, who are interacting with these travelers. This can be a toxic combination, but one that can be remedied if we give some advanced thought to it.

If an airport's workforce is not happy, there's a higher probability that the traveler will pick up on that, and if the research on emotional contagion is to be believed, it will impact their outlook in a negative manner. This negativity can naturally lead to travelers being more impatient and on the lookout for more negative things than positive ones.

It's imperative that airports do what they can to create a workplace environment that is more prone to fostering positive employee experience than negative ones. At the very least, it will help provide the traveler with a more positive experience, but even more so, it will help create a workspace that is more welcoming and inviting. Because emotions can spread among employees rather quickly, and from employees to travelers, as well as from travelers to employees, it is important to have in place measures to address the unforeseen circumstances that help generate negative emotions.

This is one of the reasons I believe Exceptionally Human communication is especially important in airports because airport executives and managers often cannot offer their people large financial rewards but they can make sure their people feel heard, acknowledged and valued. Being extra responsive to people when they look stressed out or are acting as if they are having a bad day will go a long way to reducing their stress, and it will help front line workers pay it forward to the stressed travelers they meet on the job.

It will also help avoid the opposite problem. When we block out or ignore a person's stress, we allow them to create their own story about our lack of response, which can lead to all kinds of misperceptions and misunderstandings. When we let them in, exceptionally positive interactions arise from even the smallest moments.

Is The Person Seeking Understanding? Solutions? Or Both?

It's probably fair to say that problem-solving conversations are a common communication practice at all airports. When you are engaged in problem-solving conversations, a good question to ask ourselves is what does the other person want from the conversation? It is often stated that when women discuss problems they are looking for understanding, not solutions, and that when men talk about problems, they are looking for solutions not understanding. Well, take all that gender stereotyping and throw it out the window, as it can only lead to trouble; I know plenty of women who want solutions and plenty of men who want understanding. The more important point, though, is that in problem-solving conversations people will want understanding, solutions or some combination of the two. The trick here is how to figure out which one is desired, for if we can do that, our credibility goes up.

One thing you could potentially do is ask directly if the other person wants a solution or if they simply want to be listened to for the sake of being listened to. That could work, however, there are times when a person won't know which one they want, and asking the question could possibly lead to some frustration toward us, diminishing our credibility. Also, as we know, there are countless times when the problems that occur at an airport don't have any immediate solution available, which can make the question moot. Another tack, and I would argue a safer one, would be to begin with aiming for understanding. If someone really wanted understanding and you instead started by providing solutions, the immediate pullback would be harder to rein in than if you did the opposite. Going directly for solutions could cause the person to begin feeling as though what they are experiencing doesn't matter, and once you start to go down that road, regaining trust can be difficult. If someone wants solutions and you provide understanding, they may initially be a bit frustrated, but their feelings won't necessarily be hurt. And they would probably then ask you for a solution with little to no damage to the relationship.

Staying in the moment shows true, focused attention on the other person and your credibility rises in their eyes. You are in essence saying to them, "You matter to me." Consider staying more focused on the present moment and less on how to solve the problems. Although solutions may seem readily apparent, best to err on the side of caution and fully investigate the problem to assure what solutions are actually needed.

Are We Focused on Ourselves or on Other People?

Here's an exercise for you. The next time you have a conversation with someone, ask yourself afterward if you have shared more about yourself or have you discovered more about the other person. My guess is that there is a strong probability that you won't be able to accurately answer this question, as it's not something we often think about.

However, in learning to answer this question, we can tap into something quite powerful. Because in this day and age of iThis and iThat, of customization, options and personalization, we are probably more self-concerned than ever, and probably feel even more justified than ever in being so. We love ourselves, and there's absolutely nothing wrong with that. Problems begin when we forget that there are other people too, and that other people love to be loved as well. This is not to say that we start loving everybody, but rather that if we can begin to shift our focus slightly more on other people, the results can be quite positively surprising.

> *...if we can begin to shift our focus slightly more on other people, the results can be quite positively surprising.*

Have you ever had a situation in which you are sharing something that recently happened to you and the other person replies, "Oh, I've had the same thing happen to me," or "Oh yeah, let me tell you about a time when something similar occurred with me." This is called stage-hogging, and not only is it considered an ineffective listening practice, it can also be quite damaging. What's tricky about this is that everyone does it. And you don't do it because you are so self-absorbed you cannot get beyond yourself, but you do it because you believe it's a way of connecting or creating common ground with the person you are listening to. But what is actually happening is you are placing your experience before theirs, and this can be quite agitating to the other person, and in their agitation with you, your credibility is diminished.

You gain credibility by prioritizing others and putting aside your own need to share or tell about yourself. Prioritizing others makes them feel that you value them, that they are important and interesting, and considering the investment people make to be at an airport, it's a wise choice to make. You are seen as a person to trust and talk to. That means you need to be extra-conscious about what you say. Are your words self-focused or other-focused? Are you sharing more about yourself, and as a result, discovering less about them, or are you placing yourself aside just enough so other people have the necessary space to share about themselves? This can be especially true when trying to get increased engagement from your workforce. Ask specific questions about them, or if discussing a particular subject, issue or topic, request their input or feedback. The goal here is to get others to know that you truly desire to know more about them.

The Word "I" Versus The Word "You"

Another effective way to increase your credibility

has to do with your pronoun usage in written correspondence such as email. To this end, consider how often you use the pronoun "I" in your communication compared to the pronoun "you." What is the ratio of "I" versus "you" usage? In other words, do you generally or strategically use one pronoun more than the other? I'm bringing this up because research conducted by Dr. James Pennebaker at the University of Texas at Austin uncovered some intriguing findings regarding pronoun usage. In his work, Dr. Pennebaker found that people who use the pronoun "I" more often in written correspondence are perceived to be more self-centered and self-absorbed than those who used the pronoun "you" or no pronouns at all. For example, if a colleague sends you an email asking about a particular work-related challenge they are experiencing and you reply, "I think that what I would do in the situation…," you are sending the message that you are overly self-focused and that you filter everything through yourself. Now, this is not a judgment, but rather an insight into the power of pronoun usage. If you were to instead reply, "This situation seems difficult for you. Are you asking for advice, support or suggestions as to what you can do?". The focus then remains solidly on the other person. Interestingly enough, Pennebaker's research also uncovered that people who use the pronoun "I" less frequently are often in higher status positions, whereas people who use the pronoun "I" with greater frequency are in lower status positions.

Most important to recognize, when we overuse the pronoun, "I," especially in email communication because there is an enormous interpretative gap, we can come off as sounding more self-interested or self-involved, and therefore lose some credibility. Keep in mind that for most of us, our favorite word is our own first name and that our favorite subject is often ourselves. As a result, consider using the pronoun "you" when possible, as it shifts the focus away from self and on to others. By using the pronoun "you" more than "I" in written and oral communication, we keep the focus on the other person, helping that person feel more valued. In doing so, we once again create an opportunity to increase our credibility. *Ethos* is the foundation for all truly effective communication exchanges. By applying the techniques described in this chapter, we will begin to strengthen our credibility amongst our airport colleagues, staff, stakeholders, and travelers, opening the door to deepening trust as well. And once we have our credibility house in order, we become that much more Exceptionally Human. Now we can begin to focus on what is perhaps one of the most slippery aspects of the human condition — emotions or *pathos*.

Chapter 5

Emotions *Are* The Message

"Without access to our emotions, our rational processes are handicapped, and we become little better than a conglomeration of arbitrary and random behaviors."
–Julie Schwartz Gottman and John Gottman

Airports are emotional places and emotions are powerful. Sometimes, emotions and airports can combine to turn a mature adult human being into a whining toddler in a matter of seconds. But airports can also bring out a sweet, compassionate side in even the most hardened individual. In communication, the most powerful emotions are the ones we generate in other people. These emotions affect how we are perceived, how our messages are received and how people respond to us before we even say a word. As Michelle Garcia Winner and Pamela Crooke astutely point out in their book, *Social Thinking at Work*, "Attempting to interpret each other's emotions is as much a part of the workday as doing our actual jobs."

We've all had interactions at the airport that have left us feeling worse than we did before. These interactions can have a significant impact on our well-being and how we perceive the city where the airport is located. They can also affect how we view the other people there. When we experience positive emotions, our ability to tolerate an airport's unpredictable moments is far greater than when we experience negative emotions. When our emotional experience is tied to a particular person or event, it creates a lasting impact. How the person or event is perceived, for better or worse, can result in prolonged negative associations that take tremendous time, energy and effort to undo. Sometimes these negative associations are merely annoying. Sometimes they are catastrophic.

Why Are Emotions So Powerful?

"Many airline passengers are displaying more air travel anxiety than ever before. Keeping it dormant, therefore, is indeed a challenge, as between 20% - 40% of people experience some anxiety about flying."

-Joyce A. Hunter and Jason R. Lambert

Emotions Are the Message

We all agree that emotions are powerful and have powerful effects on our interactions with other people, particularly in an airport setting. A fascinating question is *why* are they so powerful? To answer that question, the pioneer work of the psychologist Albert Ellis is worth exploring.

Ellis was the creator of Rational Emotive Behavioral Therapy. He discovered that the world of our experiences is composed of three things: facts, interpretations and emotions. Facts are those things are can be objectively agreed upon. For instance, it is a *fact* that the northern hemisphere is tilted away from the sun during the winter. *Interpretations* are the judgments or meanings we give to certain facts. In the case of winter, one could deem it to be pleasant or undesirable. *Emotions* are how we feel about the facts. And, because facts are interpreted, how we feel about something is utterly dependent on how we interpret it. So if we find winter to be enjoyable, then the emotions we experience regarding it are positive ones. On the other hand, if we interpret winter to be negative, our emotions about it will be negative as well. Coming from someone who spent practically his entire life on the seasonally temperate West Coast, you might guess how I initially felt about East Coast winters.

Now, the key to Ellis' work is how much time our minds spend in the world of fact versus the world of interpretation. How much time do you believe you spend in that world? Is it 50-50? Might you spend 30 percent of your time in facts and 70 percent in interpretation? Is it the reverse? What Ellis discovered is that we spend about 90 percent of our time in interpretations and only 10 percent in facts. Loosely speaking, 90 percent of the time we are the greatest Hollywood scriptwriters on earth, and the script we are writing is the story of our life. How we write that story dictates the emotions we experience. And the same goes for everyone else, reinforcing the fact that we have little control over other people's perceptions. It is important to know where we do have some control and exercise it.

> *Loosely speaking, 90 percent of the time we are the greatest Hollywood scriptwriters on earth...*

"It Must Be a Louisville Thing"

The following story makes this point. On a recent work trip to do some customer experience training programs at Louisville International Airport, my afternoon flight arrived 15 minutes early and I thought "Hooray!" I was looking forward to checking out the town and the extra time was much appreciated. As we approached the gate, the airplane stopped and we waited. We waited. We waited. After a few minutes, the pilot announced that due to our early arrival, the ground crew was not ready, but he assured us they would be there in a few minutes. No problem, we were early to begin with so a few minutes was really no big deal.

So, we waited. We waited. We waited. After a good 20 minutes passed, we were still waiting on the plane just short of the gate. Again, the captain announced he was waiting for the ground crew and that he had radioed everyone he could about the situation. Then he said, "This same thing happened to us last week, so I guess it's just a Louisville thing." Ouch! A Louisville thing? That cannot be interpreted as a good thing.

Now, none of us on the plane knew the reasons for the delay. There might have been very good reasons. Louisville might have an excellent record of ground crews arriving when the flights arrive and getting people and baggage off planes quickly. The people who work on the ground crews might really care about their jobs and doing them well. But all we knew was we were waiting and while we were waiting, we used the time to tell ourselves stories about why we were waiting. And the pilot not only mentally wrote his story, he actually shared it with us.

The following day while conducting my training program at the airport, I told this story and just about everyone in the room had the same reaction: They squirmed in their seats and their faces contorted, as everyone immediately understood the magnitude of the pilot's words. Was it right? Not really. Was it fair? No. Did it have an impact? It probably did for the passengers on that plane. People remember how you made them feel long after they forget what you did to make them feel that way — for both negative emotions and positive ones. Given an airport's role in the region, its economic impact and the immediate connection people make with it and a particular geographic place, it's imperative to find ways to engage the workforce and take proactive steps to ensure that a negative event does not diminish the entire airport experience.

The story definitely had an impact on the airport staff sitting in that room, even though none of them were involved in, or responsible for, the delay at the gate. They felt the emotions of the story personally though they were not personally involved.

Emotions color everything. Emotions color how we think and what we see. They allow us to feel deeply about someone, but at the same time they can blind us to certain aspects of that person. While under the influence of strong emotions, our perceptions become tainted, and our ability to see a clear picture becomes tainted as well. We can all recall the power of falling in love and how when we are under the influence of those fabulous emotions, our

> *Emotions color everything.*

behaviors can become less than rational (What's the big deal in taking another personal day?). The same goes when we are experiencing the power of anger or resentment — our rationality becomes suspect.

Simply put, the power of emotions to affect how people respond to our messages is enormous — both positively and negatively. Exceptionally Human communicators can create the desired emotions in others.

The Emotions We Expect To Feel Influence Us Too

"Customers who receive poor customer service will be unhappy and experience negative emotions such as anger or fear. Customers who receive smiling customer service will be happier and experience positive emotions."

–Joyce A. Hunter and Jason R. Lambert

Let's add another wrinkle to this dynamic. Research suggests that the emotions we expect to feel have a strong influence on the emotions we actually end up feeling. For example, if we expect to be disappointed by another person, we will look for information that confirms that expectation. When we expect to be satisfied with a person, we look for reasons to be so. It is an idiosyncratic feature of our brilliant minds that we desire to feel a particular way based upon past experience and then "write a story" for ourselves that justifies feeling that way.

Think about this in terms of airports with the words of Professor Schaberg who I quoted at the beginning of this book in mind: "At the airport no one cares about you; they just want your credit card; they just want to see you shuffle along and leave this space." We agreed this opinion isn't true or fair but it is still the expectation many people have when they walk into the airport. Think about the story of Dr. David Dao who was forcibly removed from his seat and dragged off his flight at Chicago's O'Hare International Airport in the spring of 2017. Video footage of this incident circulated around social media and traditional news outlets like wildfire, spurring outrage from people everywhere. This was a single horrifying and extremely unusual incident but it still powerfully shaped people's expectations about how they will be treated when they travel.

This means that the negative feelings people had about us last week or last year influence how they receive our messages today, which is bad news. On the other hand, positive feelings from the past also influence how people receive our messages, which is good news. Perhaps the best news, though, is that unless people have done significant reading about emotions, they probably have little insight into why they feel a particular way. They just feel it. This gives us opportunities to use simple techniques that create positive emotional interactions with people that satisfy them and satisfy us, which can greatly influence how travelers and airport workers experience us. Let's talk about some of these techniques right now.

"I" Versus "You" Again — with a Twist!

We know that the words we choose have big impact on how people hear our messages. In Chapter 4, we talked about how using the pronoun "you" instead of "I" in our communication with others makes us sound less self-centered and self-absorbed and so increases our credibility.

This is not an absolute rule, however. There are situations in which using the pronoun "you" can actually damage our credibility and cause others to experience negative emotions ranging from defensiveness to anger. In what is known as the *Language of Responsibility*, the use of "you" during disagreements or in situations when things don't go according to plan can lead other people to feel as though you are solely blaming them and not taking responsibility yourself, which then leads to negative emotions.

People tend to feel better when blame is not being directly assigned to them. Our use of the pronoun "I" more than "you" can come across as being self-accountable and taking responsibility, which will lower people's defenses. When we overuse the pronoun "you" versus "I," we are perceived as less accountable or responsible and more of a finger-pointer, increasing the chances others will become more defensive. So we need to be careful that when we use "you" in these situations, we also use "I" to create a sense of balance.

Understanding Others Versus Being Understood Ourselves

Another step we can take toward generating positive emotions in people is how we prioritize those people. This brings us back to a key question: What is more important — understanding others or being understood by others?

Think about conversations you've had where there was an underlying misunderstanding. Do you have a tendency to want to make yourself understood first, before understanding the other person's position? If you are like most people, including me, you probably find yourself wanting to be understood first. I think it's safe to say that most people fall into this category, especially travelers. We all want to be understood and will take whatever steps are necessary to make that happen. At the same time, how often have you pressed and pressed to be understood, only to find yourself feeling frustrated because you have not been able to get the other person to see where you are coming from? Not only that, how many times have you been in the position of wanting to be understood only to find the other person is doing nothing more than trying to get you to understand them, such as the airline ticket counter representative flatly explaining baggage fees to a puzzled passenger who now finds himself out $50? And when that occurs, how does he feel? Frustrated? Angry? Disappointed? Probably so, and this significantly impacts how he now perceives the other person, both in terms of how he feels about the other person, but also the credibility he assigns to that individual.

You can see the point — this dynamic works both ways. In those times we are trying diligently to be understood, we may very well be generating negative emotions in others that will significantly inhibit both their ability and desire to understand us. The point being, in those instances when we want to be Exceptionally Human communicators, or really anytime, prioritize understanding the other person first, even if that means we ourselves are not being understood right away.

By making sure you understand why a particular issue or subject is important to a traveler, airport worker, colleague or subordinate, that person will feel listened to, which in turn has them feeling better about you than otherwise might happen. This will increase the possibility that in turn they will desire to understand where you stand. Consider working a bit more to understand others before attempting to be understood. When you push to have yourself understood, you may have their attention in the short run, but you are asking them to delay expressing themselves, which may cause them to feel less important and in turn take what you have to say less seriously. If this sounds familiar, it should. Making other people feel important is one of the key points from the ethos chapter.

> *Consider working a bit more to understand others before attempting to be understood.*

Emotions, Stress and Safety

When people feel valued, they are more responsive to the people who value them. In a June 2017 article by Katie Scott in *Employee Benefits,* she described a situation at London City Airport where it was discovered that 22 percent of the airport workforce was living paycheck to paycheck. There was concern among airport leadership that the emotional stress generated by hanging by such a thin financial thread might impede the workers' ability to carry out their functions in a safe manner. This possibility was a lose-lose for everyone. In response to this, the airport rolled out a financial well-being strategy that included a gamification-style savings app to help airport workers with finding ways to save money. The thinking was that if employees felt more financially secure, their stress would be reduced, reducing the possibility for workplace accidents and increasing their sense of well being. As a result of the airport's efforts, there was "an 18% increase in the proportion of employees providing a positive response to the statement: 'London City Airport cares about my health and well being.'" This feeling of being cared about is an emotional response to how these employees were communicated with, and in this case, the rolling out of a savings program told them that they were valued indeed. How well this translates to less workplace accidents remains to be seen, but one undeniable upside is that these employees feel better about their workplace than they had prior to this savings program, which is a win-win for everyone.

Consistency Versus Variability in Communication Style

It is often said that being consistent is an admirable trait. Whether the consistency has to do with our character or our communication style, we think being consistent leads to higher credibility. Nobody wants to be viewed as one who waffles or is a flip-flopper, as we so often hear political candidates point out about his or her rivals. As it is for products, so it is for people and our relationships with them: Consistency is the key to building loyalty and trust. So it makes good sense that we would want to be consistent at an airport, as it increases our credibility in the eyes of travelers and the workforce. However, there are times when being consistent will actually work against us, and this is especially true in our communications with others.

Each of us has our own preferred communication style. Be it assertive, passive, aggressive or accommodating, our style is preferred because it's familiar, we have success with it, it causes us little discomfort and it requires little effort. Simply put, it's something we can do without much thought. Now, there's nothing wrong with this approach whatsoever. And at the same time, just because our preferred style works for us does not mean it will work well for others. Our accommodating style may cause others to feel annoyed, confused or some other undesirable emotion, and if we are attempting to be an Exceptionally Human communicator in that moment, we'll fail if we don't adapt our style. It goes back to those characteristics of the competent communicator. The competent communicator has access to an entire range of communication styles and the ability to perform those styles when needed. They are equally able to be assertive and amenable. The key is, whatever style you choose should be selected with the intention of generating a desired emotional response in the other person. To that end, we need to be aware of other people's preferred style, and most importantly, how they like to be communicated with.

When you adapt your communication style to other people's preferred style, people feel more comfortable and relaxed around you. And it increases the probability of positively impacting how they feel about you, as well as their receptivity to your message. Having a set or rigid style runs the risk of doing just the opposite. Being more adaptable with your communication style will take effort on your part. First, you need to know what your preferred style is. You also need to note what styles you are uncomfortable with, as those are the styles you want to practice. Take one uncomfortable style and practice it twice a day for three weeks. If you are assertive, practice taking a step back, and if you are more inclined to be shy, practice being more assertive. Note how you feel employing that style, what is challenging about it, and what you do to overcome it. After three weeks, you'll find this style will begin to feel more comfortable and more accessible to you when you need it.

Focus on the Goal —
But at What Cost?

You know how it goes. When a deadline is fast approaching, you begin to feel the stress, as do others who are working with you. So our interactions become more efficient. Gone are salutations and unnecessary words — we cut right to the point. Our reading becomes less effective as well, as we start quickly scanning our emails, looking just for the information that will help meet the goal. And in this process, people might begin to feel slighted, diminished and minimized, all as a result of how they are being communicated with. Although the goal is reached, the fallout from those negative emotions leads to greater resistance and distance in future interactions. And it's not just when deadlines approach — at an airport, stress can unfold at just about any time for countless reasons, and our response to that stress will follow suit. It's human to do this, and not necessarily anyone's fault, but it doesn't need to be that way.

Our first step when we are in stressful situations is to place greater value on the relationship. We are not necessarily placing less value on the goal; we are simply not letting achieving the goal compromise the relationship. We are all subject to curt behavior, outbursts and sharp exchanges, and those won't necessarily disappear. At the same time, the more effort we place in cultivating our relationships with those we work with — airport colleagues, partners or stakeholders — or our travelers, the more valued they begin to feel, and the more positive emotions they actually experience in relation to us. In building up that good will, we not only establish allies along the way, we earn their forgiveness in advance when stress causes us to behave in less than desirable ways.

Even though achieving a goal is ultimately necessary, damaging relationships in the process can be more harmful in the long run. By making sure people know their contributions matter and that they are valued throughout the process, you increase their buy-in. Give them positive feedback when it's warranted or when it's not expected. No need to be Pollyannaish, just take a few extra minutes to nurture relationships to keep others feeling positive about you. When you prioritize the goal over the relationship, you may alienate the very people you need to work with you, and in the process reduce opportunities for future collaboration. Keeping those emotions as positive as possible is the key to being Exceptionally Human.

In Written Communication, Don't Let Emotional Tone Get Lost!

An oft-quoted statistic from Dr. Albert Mehrabian states that more than 90 percent of the meaning in a verbal exchange is derived independent of the words themselves. It's not what you say but how you say it that matters most. In the recent past, a significantly larger portion of our workplace communication took place either face to face or over the phone where it was much easier to convey emotional tones – especially positive ones. Nowadays, face-to-face exchanges are far less frequent and are more often replaced by electronic communication. The meaning intended by the sender and construed by the receiver in texts, social media, instant messages and emails may be lost in the written word, which often lacks tone and feeling.

Unlike verbal communication, which has interpretative gaps of its own, what we write has interpretative gaps as big as the Grand Canyon in comparison. That's because the most significant nonverbal quality of what we say is our *emotional tone*. Emotional tone is the overall feel of a message. That feel can be supportive, abrasive, warm, cold, friendly or provocative, to name a few. Verbal communication includes not only the words we choose,

> *Emotional tone is the overall feel of a message.*

Emotions Are the Message

but also our volume, rate, pitch and emphasis, or lack thereof. In verbal communication, people hear our tone and have an immediate emotional response to it.

In written communication, given our real voice is absent, it's our composition style, the words we choose, our punctuation and grammar — even whether or not we use bold letters. All these allow people to fill in the blanks, make interpretations and then feel whatever it is they are going to feel. And if we are trying to be Exceptionally Human communicators, the feeling we desire is positive. So, how can we communicate positivity? We can place ourselves in others' emotional shoes and ask ourselves, "How might the way I'm communicating this cause *them* to feel?" Note how it's not about how we think we would feel, but rather how they might feel. In doing this, we are simultaneously placing our focus on them so they feel valued, while we are also increasing our credibility in their eyes. It's all interrelated.

When you are conscious of your emotional tone in a written message you have taken the recipient's feelings into consideration. The how of what you say gives you a higher probability of having your message received by others in the way you intended. This is not about being touchy-feely or politically correct, this is about being strategic. Staying conscious helps bring people closer to you, as they will feel more comfortable communicating with you, even when the subject matter is difficult. By placing insufficient attention on your emotional tone, you may be inadvertently pushing people away from you, because they may find the tone of your message off putting. Although this takes additional effort, the practice will allow you to keep people engaged, even if the subject matter is disagreeable. To recognize how this works, consider the tone difference between reading the word "Thanks" versus "Thanks!" They read differently, do they not? They feel different. That's the power of tone.

> *"Thanks" versus "Thanks!"*

Keeping these *pathos* techniques in mind allows us to be Exceptionally Human with our communication and generates desirable emotions in others. These techniques include using the word "I" in conversations about responsibility, focusing on understanding other people before being understood and adapting our communication style to the style of the people we meet. Other important techniques involve emphasizing both the goal and the relationship when working with people and paying close attention to how people might read the emotional tone of our written communications, making sure the tone they read is positive. Practicing these techniques will help ensure your communication and your airport is that much more Exceptionally Human!

Chapter 6

Logically Speaking

"Give me a reason to love you."
–Portishead

*"Purpose is often misunderstood…
It's not a goal but a reason."*
–L. Hill, G. Brandeau, E. Truelove,
and K. Lineback, Collective Genius

In the two previous chapters, we stressed the importance of establishing our credibility to generate a desired emotional response within all who occupy our airport space. It's vitally important that we frame our communication properly so that it can be digested easily. Logic and reason are what allow us to do just that.

Logic and reason ground and contextualize our communication: Logic and reason can are also powerful tools so the other person can derive the meaning that most reflects what we desire to say. And that meaning must be appropriate to the other person. Again, it's not about us, it's about them — better yet, their perceptions. No matter how reasonable and rational we might find our communication, it must correlate with what the other person finds reasonable, rational, and appropriate, or it simply will not work. If you've ever tried explaining to a traveler the reason their flight is delayed has something to do with weather elsewhere, then you know what I mean. If what we convey is seen as inappropriate, we begin to erode the very credibility we worked to establish, and begin to generate emotions that will cause the other person to be less inclined to listen to us.

Nothing is guaranteed. Think about how many times you thought you knew what someone else meant when later on you came to discover the meaning was much different than you thought. To err is human, and we err constantly when it comes to our communication, either as the sender or receiver of messages. Don't feel bad about it, simply accept it. By dropping the judgment, you can view these errors as facts in and of themselves, and begin to strategize how to do something about it. You can apply sound reason and logic so your communications are properly contextualized. As they say in real estate — location, location, location! In communication it's context, context, context!

Like all the skills required to become Exceptionally Human communicators, excellence in the skills of *logos, or reason*, is required. All of us have struggled to write clear, concise, complete and compelling messages in our lives, at work or in our private lives. Some of us have even worked to write books, and I can tell you from first-hand experience, it is a struggle.

Like the skills needed to build trust and generate desired emotions, all of us already possess the ability to express facts and reasons, yet all of us have the ability to be even better at it. We just need to focus on six areas. The first is making sure we understand other people's facts and reasons first through the technique of **active listening**. The second is to grasp the **context** of the communication. The third is making sure everything we write and say is **relevant** to the task at hand. The fourth is to avoid ambiguity by being **clear and specific**. The fifth is to avoid using logical fallacies and instead use **sound logic**. And the sixth is to provide an appropriate level of **detail**.

Understand People's Facts First Through Active Listening

The first step to expressing compelling facts and reasons is to make sure we clearly understand what people want or need from an interaction. We all know what it is like to get this part of communication wrong. For example, if you've ever thought your spouse asked you to stop by the grocery store on your way home when she actually said to come home and watch the kids so she could find some peace grocery shopping, you'll know what I mean. Or consider an airport employee who is required to remain at the airport beyond his shift time, and when he offers a complaint, is given the response, "That's just how it is." Often, we believe we listened to a person, when in fact we have only heard them — this distinction will be made clear in Chapter 7. We all have listening challenges, and it is as human as breathing to not listen as well as we can, but there is something we can do about it. In the Appendix, we'll get into details on how to develop your **active listening** skills.

The Context Rules All

Context is the **who**, **what**, **when**, **where** and **why** of our communications. Context has a powerful influence on the facts and reasons in our messages, and it is powerful in part because it is often invisible. Context tends to be implicit in our messages rather than explicit. Context is about the assumptions we make about the message we are sending — and as we all know, wrong assumptions lead to wrong messages. When talking to people working at the airport, we must ask ourselves what agency do they work for, what is their position or rank, at what point in their shift are they, and are they having a good or bad day. Some questions are about the airport itself — is it a busy or slow time, are there many delays, or are all operations running fairly smoothly. Context impacts everything.

There is a classic communications exercise that demonstrates how context, or lack thereof, powerfully influences our assumptions. The exercise features a photo of an elderly woman crying. The initial look at this photo is very close up on the woman's face. When people are asked to describe how she is feeling, they more often than not say she is upset, sad or grieving. The next shot is taken a bit further away, and we see the same woman crying in front of what looks to be the door of a church. Again, when asked what this woman is feeling, people use similar adjectives. The next photo is a much wider view, and the woman is one of several people in front of a church where a wedding party is departing. This time around, folks say that the woman is happy, crying tears of joy, and nobody thinks she's sad anymore. That is the power of context and what happens when we make assumptions.

Many times, we understand the context of a message so well we do not need to think about it. When a friend texts, "Wanna get a coffee?", we know which coffee shop she means. We know she wants to get the coffee right now. We know she probably only wants to take ten minutes to drink the coffee. We know it is a casual offer we can decline if we are busy at that moment. And our friend knows we know these things. On the other hand, if our boss texts us "Can you meet me at the coffee shop in Terminal A in ten minutes?" during the workday — when both of us are in the office — that's a whole different context and it dictates a different response.

Or think about this example. If we tell a complete stranger to follow our exact directions, they may think we are crazy and ignore us. If we tell them to follow our exact directions because we are wearing an airport security badge or uniform, they are going to pay more attention to us because they now understand the context of our message. And if we are wearing the uniform of a public safety officer (exuding *ethos*/credibility), and we are speaking in a calm and authoritative manner (generating *pathos*/emotions), people will not only listen to us, they will do what we ask.

So we should take a moment to think about the who, what, when, where, and why of our messages, particularly the important ones. We should make sure we understand the context before we proceed communicating with the fatigued traveler, the grumpy employee or the under appreciated custodial worker. It can make a tremendous difference in the effectiveness of what we say, and more importantly, its receptivity.

Is Our Message Relevant to the Task at Hand?

At airports, as it is with most workplaces, we often find ourselves in situations when there is a specific task that needs completing in a very compressed time period. If we are working with others on this task, our communication might vary. In situations like this, some of us like to keep our communication restricted simply to the task at hand, while others will veer off topic as a way to release pressure and perhaps add a much-needed distraction. Both are reasonable communication approaches.

There are times when I appreciate and enjoy when the communication goes beyond the scope of the task and turns to non-related matters. There are times, especially early in a working relationship, when this can prove beneficial, as we are taking time to get to know the other person. I've found this to be particularly helpful when working with an airport's workforce on a customer service program. After spending time getting to know the participants and developing a connection with them, their receptivity to the material presented is much higher than it otherwise would be. Our task in these cases is to build a rapport with a person that is essential to a good working relationship. If the task is to brainstorm new ideas, then veering off topic is precisely the point of the communication and we want to do more of it.

However, if we talk about non-relevant issues too regularly, or if it begins to become a distraction to actually completing the task, then it becomes a liability. A lost traveler needs to know where to go, not to engage in relationship-building chit chat. When our communication sticks to the task at hand, providing relevant information and appropriate details, our positions come across as more sound, reasonable and logical, which helps to ensure successful dialogue. People feel we are respecting their time. Most of all, people will feel that we are putting their needs and interests first by limiting our messages to topics that interest them rather than just ourselves.

To illustrate, I have a friend who just loves to share what is going on not only in his life, but in the lives of all our mutual friends as well. As a matter of fact, whenever I prepare to speak with him, I have to make sure I'm allowing enough time, as these conversations are never brief. And although I often enjoy these talks, there are times when what I really want to do is get to the point, without all the unnecessary storytelling. But that never happens — and that's fine, as this is my friend and our trust has been built up over years. I simply accept it. In other situations, where trust hasn't been developed, it is a liability.

Now, there are certainly cultural factors that play into this, and given airports are spaces where multiple cultures intersect, some may appreciate taking more time to ease into a conversation, while others want to get right to the point. And beyond cultures, there are individual personalities as well. At the same time, if you start straying off topic too much, your communication effectiveness may suffer. For instance, you probably had conversations in which a person says "I had dinner with X last night and she told me the most incredible news," but then proceeds to tell you first the story of how they planned the dinner, then how much traffic they hit on the way to the restaurant and then about changes to the restaurant's menu and you are thinking, "Just tell me the news!"

In our professional airport lives, these conversations are easier to manage. One way to make sure our communication is relevant is to always offer an agenda at the beginning of a communication. This agenda does not have to be formal. You can say to a colleague, "Do you have twenty minutes to talk about issues A, B and C?" When your colleague says "yes," you know the conversation is relevant to her and you can go forward. Another simple trick I like to use is when I have three questions for a person, I send them in three short emails rather than one long email. I also clearly label the topic of each in a subject line such as "Important question about budget of Project Alpha." When the colleague opens the email, I know she has decided the topic is relevant to her.

So it is important for us to always be aware of the topic of our communication and to be strategic and thoughtful about how we approach the other person. Straying off topic, although at times not a bad thing, can dilute our logic and message and limit our ability to keep people actively engaged with us.

Clear and Specific... Or the Agonies of Ambiguity

Ideally, all our communication would be clear, specific and make sense to all people who move though our airports. I know, easier said than done! By eliminating ambiguity and providing people with a smooth and simple explanation for things, we assure they have the necessary foundation to make sense of our argument. Their willingness to accept what we have to say will increase. They will feel more grounded and at ease in our presence, and they will be more willing to stay engaged and accept difficult messages.

Keep in mind that as human beings, we are endlessly filling in the blanks as we attempt to make sense of the world around us. Over time, we become predisposed to do so in ways that are distinct to our experiences, to our expectations and to our preferences. As part of our way to avoid uncertainty, we like to ascribe meaning to things, circumstances and situations as quickly as possible. As a general rule, we like to avoid uncertainty, which is why when someone communicates something that doesn't make sense, we become less engaged, as we don't want to be burdened with uncertainty. And, given that airports can be hotbeds of uncertainty, we must bear this in mind.

By grounding our communication in meaning and giving others a clear reason or rationale, we help them avoid the uncomfortable feelings associated with uncertainty, the stress that it can produce and the impact it can have on their well being. When people are feeling anxious, nervous or unsettled, they view information through that lens and it will absolutely taint how they ascribe meaning to it. Sometimes this may be to a strategic advantage, but this book isn't about that, it's about recognizing these human aspects so we can best convey information and connect with others.

If we go back to the work of Albert Ellis, when he states how 90 percent of the time we are making up stories about 10 percent of the facts, you can see how significant specificity is. The fewer facts you provide people, the more inclined they will be to make up stories that fit their perspectives, which may not necessarily be ours. So, what can you do to help assure those stories are told in the way you would like, or at the very least increase the odds of that actually happening?

> *Give people additional clear and specific facts.*

Simple. Give people additional clear and specific facts. Most importantly, attend to their point of view, not yours.

One simple technique that enhances clarity and specificity is to use numbers in messages whenever possible. Quantities, measures, prices, times and dates are all easy candidates for this approach.

Some examples include:

Vague: "We are having a lot of people traveling Thanksgiving weekend and we need everyone to do their part."

Specific: "We are having a 20 percent increase in passenger volume on Thanksgiving weekend, so please be extra patient and understanding with everyone you interact with during this time."

Vague: "The budget for this project is tight."

Specific: "The budget for this project is $3,500 less than we expected, so we'll be reprioritizing our goals and establish new ones by week's end."

Vague: "Come by my office anytime after Tuesday."

Specific: "Come next Wednesday, January 19 between 2 and 3 pm"

Another simple technique is to ask ourselves what the other person already knows about a topic. It's human to assume that people know the facts that we know, or to forget that they don't know these facts yet. For example, in spite of all the TSA information available online, many travelers will attempt to bring items through the security checkpoints that are clearly prohibited (recall the family's peanut butter story). This can cause some additional grief and stress on both the traveler and the TSA employee. Bearing this in mind, providing a bit more leeway in terms of what each party can expect from each other can help reduce the tension in these moments.

One of the other advantages of being clear and specific is that it helps people be clear and specific with us in return. When we say, "The budget is $3,500," it makes it easier for the other person to say, "I can work with that," or he can explain that he "really needs $4,000 for this job." When we are specific, we are better communicators and we help make other people better communicators too.

Logical and Persuasive

Clear and specific facts are the foundation on which we build reasons why people should agree with us and take the actions we propose. Even better, compelling facts make persuasion simple. Like most businesses, airports spend their time and money on something new only when they are convinced of the likelihood of a worthwhile return on investment, or when the risk is balanced by a commensurate potential return. People don't invest in things they think are bad ideas; they only invest in good ideas. (Whether the perceived good idea actually turns out to be good is another matter, of course!)

The same is true in our personal lives. If our partner says to us, "Let's go to the Caribbean this February. We hate winter!" We might reply, "I don't know." If she says, "I found this four-star resort. It has tennis and snorkeling for me. Yoga and surfing for you. A pool and water-slide for the kids. And it has a great deal right now." We would be far more inclined to say yes. One technique I use to test the persuasiveness of my arguments is to ask myself this simple question: if I were the other person and this were the proposal I received and for these reasons, would I agree with it? If my answer is "No" then I know I have more work to do.

When I am on the other side of the question, and

I'm the person who is on the receiving end of an argument, I am always on the lookout for logical fallacies or what we call BS in casual conversation. The world is filled with smooth talkers and likeable sociopaths, (think Bernie Madoff or any other con artist) who use flawed logic to get ahead by harming us. We don't want to be these kinds of people, and we don't want to use their tricks. Although their methods might work initially, they will certainly backfire on us once exposed.

One common fallacy, or false logic, is the **red herring**. A red herring is when someone begins to provide very reasonable, sound information about a particular subject that in fact has very little to do with the matter at hand. Think of those political candidates who provide an eloquent response to a question that totally avoids answering the question and there you have it.

Some other notable fallacies include the **slippery slope**, which is when someone takes the position that if one particular event happens, it will lead to a cascading effect, either good or bad. The **false dilemma** is when one presents only two possible options, when, in fact, there are several options available. The **hasty generalization** is when we make broad, sweeping statements based upon a significantly small sample of information available.

There are more, but those are the most common. The thing about fallacies is that credibility and feelings can overshadow the most common ones so they go unnoticed. If we go back to Bernie Madoff, he had this amazing perceived credibility. And because people felt opportunities to have him invest their money were rare, they jumped at the opportunity. Incidentally, this is another classic fallacy, that of **scarcity**. And, as we all know, what at first appeared to be too good to be true was in fact just that. But under the right circumstances, it was initially taken as the opposite. Do your best to be mindful to eliminate fallacies in your own logic, and always build arguments that would pass your most stringent standards.

The Right Level of Detail Is…What?

Often a major culprit in ineffective communication is the omission of details and important information. In our warp-speed age of information transference, we try to make our communication as efficient and succinct as possible. Consider the number of 1-2 sentence email correspondence we have sent and received, not to mention those wonderfully brief Twitter and text exchanges. And although there's nothing inherently wrong with brevity, if we simply remain succinct, we may not be adequately providing the necessary background information and pertinent details needed to assure mutual understanding.

When it comes to providing a solid grounding for others, a safer bet is to err on the side of more, not less. When you share pertinent details, you help to create a more logical and grounded argument, ensuring others understand where you are coming from and where you are going, while minimizing misunderstandings. Consider regularly sharing details. When you fail to let people know where you are coming from or where you are going, your logic can appear less sound, increasing the chances for misunderstandings. Your interactions in turn are less effective and productive, and credibility suffers.

At the same time, this advice requires us to answer two tricky questions: what are the pertinent details in the communication? And especially, what are the details the other person considers pertinent?

Just as Exceptionally Human communicators adapt their communication style to the style of their receivers, they also need to calibrate the amount of detail they share to the amount of detail the receiver wants. We have all encountered the "big picture" person who tells us "I trust you. Go do it and don't bother me, just deliver the results you promise." We have all also encountered the "detail fiend" who says "I want to see every step along the way that gets us to the results we want." These styles are neither right nor wrong, of course. They are just the styles people want us to adopt when we are communicating with them.

Similarly, too much information can cause confusion and uncertainty just like too little information can cause confusion and uncertainty. For example, and anyone who is not especially tech savvy will appreciate this, is the experience of trying to buy a new television or computer. A friendly, enthusiastic young person greets us in the store and instantly begins to tell us numbers, speeds, acronyms, these-es and those-es and we have no idea what he's saying. These details aren't as pertinent to us, and because we don't understand them, we often leave the store with nothing more than additional confusion.

When it comes to offering pertinent details, the good news is you can always ask people what they want. You just need to make sure you put the burden of the question on yourself. "Did I explain that clearly? Have I told you everything you want to know?"

The Power of Facts

We've talked a lot in this book about how trust and emotion are powerful tools of communication and we've looked at research that suggests they may be more powerful tools than facts. We may be tempted to think that trust and emotion are the only communications tools we need. We might think that good feelings will always beat a good deal. But we'd be wrong.

Let's talk about Dr. David Dao again. When Dr. Dao was dragged off his flight at Chicago's O'Hare International Airport, consumer groups threatened to boycott United Airlines and even Capitol Hill, expressing dismay at this truly unacceptable behavior. This was it! Enough was enough! You simply cannot treat people this way!

Then, low and behold, a few months later, when United releases its quarterly earnings report, earnings were up 39 percent compared to the same quarter the previous year, as were bookings. Whoa! A 39 percent increase after dragging someone down the aisle, after communicating with someone like that. How can this be?

The reasons this can be are two cold hard facts. In a July 2017 New York Times article, Northeastern University economics professor John Kworka, Jr. stated, "It's very difficult at this point in time for consumers to exact a penalty against airlines that have exhibited poor customer service." That is to say, airline consolidation has left travelers with relatively few choices on most routes. It is hard to boycott an airline if they are the only one offering a direct flight — or any flight — from your home airport to your destination.

The second reason was given by Northwestern University Associate Professor Michael J. Mazzeo, "What the airlines have learned is the customer cares about low prices more than anything else." This means the average traveler will put up with a lot of hassle to pay the lowest price, including at least the theoretical possibility they will be physically dragged off a flight for which they have bought a ticket. That's powerful testimony to the power of reason.

In Summary

The mere fact that we are able to communicate with each other is a miracle beyond miracles. Given all those thoughts racing through our minds, the uniqueness of our experiences and our vast emotional range, being on the same page with anyone is, quite simply, amazing. That's why it's of vast importance that we do everything within our power to ensure our airport communication provides clarity.

With every airport interaction ask yourself if you are providing appropriate information, useful information and sufficient information. By making sure your communication provides clarity, you come across as more reasonable and your positions more sound. This ensures others fully understand the situation and are better prepared to engage in productive dialogue.

Logos, our reason and rationality, are of significant importance in this process. Remember though, without generating desired emotions and establishing credibility, our communications go nowhere. Back in ancient Greece, it was the philosopher Plato who championed *logos*. Logic and reason are deeply seeded in the western tradition. The Enlightenment period in 18th Century Europe employed reason to cut through monarchical and religious dogma to spawn personal and social liberation. But in and of itself, logic is not enough. Try reasoning with a 5 year old as to why they should or should not do something…good luck. Because the 5 year old is still developing their rational mind, and will be for the next 15 years or so, emotions rule the day. And as we mature and develop, and as our minds mature and develop, we can deploy reason and logic in highly impactful ways. It's in the conjunction of the 3 elements of logic, emotion, and credibility that allow us to become Exceptionally Human communicators!

Chapter 7

Why Are We Doing This? Making Exceptionally Human Communication Work for Your Airport

> *"Where does the solution already exist? Where is the future already happening in the organization right now?"*
> –M. O'Connor & B. Dornfeld,
> The Moment You Can't Ignore

As you can now tell, becoming an Exceptionally Human communicator requires focus and effort. It's the application of age-old wisdom in an amazingly fast-paced 21st Century world. Now is the time to put everything we've covered together so you can start enjoying the benefits of being an Exceptionally Human communicator. To that end, we want to recognize the places and times in which we engage in this extraordinarily powerful communication practice in our airports.

Key Organizational Interactions

In our professional lives, the most important communications are what I call **key organizational interactions**, or KOIs. In this chapter, we'll begin by exploring what KOIs are and the criteria for defining them. We'll also explore the latent value within those KOI interactions, value that is waiting to be extracted. To help demonstrate how we can actually pull all this off, I'll explore a real-life organizational situation that shows establishing credibility, generating desired emotions and applying flawless logic in action.

Do you know which of your airport interactions have the most significant impact on how your airport is perceived? Do you know the places within your airport where KOIs frequently occur, both internally and externally?

Key organizational interactions are those interactions that have the deepest impact on how people and organizations are perceived. KOIs can take place both within the airport itself or beyond the airport's walls. KOIs can be among coworkers, landside operations team members, superiors and subordinates, or between the airport and the travelers and stakeholders they serve. What differentiates KOIs from everyday interactions is KOIs tend to have a much greater and longer-lasting impact on how the airport is perceived compared to other interactions. An exchange between a stakeholder employee and their boss can be a mundane interaction. It evolves to a KOI if the boss is unnecessarily demanding or harsh in such a way that causes the employee to begin to feel negatively about the organization, and consequently, the airport. KOIs can be interactions between an hourly, front-line employee working at a retail outlet and a traveler, where an exceptionally positive interaction can outweigh dissatisfaction about having to endure check-in hassles. And the KOIs we have with our colleagues, stakeholders, partners, supervisors and travelers make a huge difference in our success.

KOIs can be subtle. The difference between being greeted warmly or being ignored when we walk through the airport is enormous. A supervisor simply acknowledging that her team feels frustrated about the work required to carry out an upcoming customer service initiative, and validating that frustration, can be the difference between that team feeling motivated and inspired to successfully drive the initiative or not. In other words, KOIs are the exchanges that will ultimately be remembered. They become the stories people recall and share with others. They tend to have Exceptionally Human qualities. These are moments of communication competence. As you'll remember, communication competence is when the manner in which we express the message is satisfying to the other person — not necessarily the substance of the message itself.

Any exchange can potentially become a KOI. Here are but a few airport examples:
- exchanges between airport management and stakeholder employees
- exchanges between airport staff and various airline personnel
- exchanges between wheelchair assistants and family members
- interactions between custodial staff, frontline and travelers
- interactions between custodial staff and other airport employees
- interactions between travelers and skycaps at the curbside
- interactions between employee parking lot bus driver and airport workers
- interactions at security checkpoints
- exchanges among colleagues
- social media postings

Don't overlook them. They appear all the time! The ASQ Survey is a good place to look when attempting to locate KOIs. Take a few moments now to list some possible KOIs specific to your organization.

Exceptionally Positive KOIs in the "Value Zone"

CEO and author Vineet Nayar coined the term "Value Zone." Nayar focuses on the Value Zone of large retail businesses in his book *Employees First, Customers Second*. His insights are equally compelling and essential at the airport. The Value Zone is the place where an organization's value is built or broken. It is where interactions between an organization's people and their clients and customers determine the true perceived value of that organization. Again, this is quite similar to what ASQ's Dimitri Coll spoke of in the forward about touch points or moments of truth. Success in the Value Zone is essential to people and organizations who want to thrive in a world where the internet, robust e-commerce, automated manufacturing, sophisticated analytical algorithms and globalization are all powerful competition. Exceptionally Human communication in positive KOIs builds the Value Zone. KOIs and Exceptionally Human communication cannot be outsourced or performed by computers. And more, within the Value Zone the potential for fantastic amounts of new value to be created exists, if we can just see the opportunities!

Nayar stresses the importance of, you guessed it, an organization putting its employees first and its customers second. Customers are still a high priority, of course, and at an airport it is an imperative. However it is the employees who reside in the Value Zone who deliver the ultimate value of the services and products that the organization provides. At airports, these people are quite often frontline employees who earn an hourly wage, experience no direct financial benefit beyond that hourly pay and are employed by numerous stakeholders and airline partners.

Some companies seem to forget how important their frontline interactions are and how important their employees are; I'm sure you have a few in mind. At the same time, some organizations intimately know the value of this Value Zone. Companies such as Whole Foods and Zappos (both of which are now owned by Amazon) come to mind, where seemingly each and every interaction with their frontline employee is one that is pleasant and leaves one feeling truly valued. The point here is that an organization's success or failure is often dependent on how well the least paid employees communicate. It is not just external exchanges, it is internal ones as well, and these companies are known to treat their employees with as much value as they do their customers. With airports it's a bit more

> ...an organization's success or failure is often dependent on how well the least paid employees communicate.

challenging, for as we know, the majority of the airport workforce is outside the airport's direct control, but nonetheless it's important to recognize.

There are multiple forms of value that can be extracted via Exceptionally Human communication. Here are just a few possible forms value can take:

- time
- motivation
- engagement
- trust
- innovation
- energy
- buy-In
- advocacy
- airport repute
- positive airport perception
- sales
- workforce physical health
- revenue
- employee empowerment
- workforce productivity
- goal attainment
- rekindled interest, loyalty
- effort
- creativity

I'm certain there are other forms of value you can

identify. Consider what a 5 percent improvement in any one of these areas would look like for you and your airport. It's not unlike having a 5 percent return on a financial investment; it's sound, reasonable, keeps you ahead of inflation and has little downside. In an 8-hour or 480-minute workday, 5 percent equals 24 minutes. How would 24 additional minutes of trust impact how your airport performs? What about 24 additional minutes of motivation or creativity? Or, what about 24 additional minutes of "Thanks!" versus "Thanks." No doubt, the effort would benefit you and your airport, and it's far more realistic to achieve 5 percent than eight hours worth. And really, communication is the key to unlocking the 5 percent, then 5 percent more and so on. Even if it's not quite 5 percent, there can still be significant impact. Recall from Dimitri Coll's forward how an increase of 1 percent in the ASQ's global passenger satisfaction mean generates, on average, a growth of NAR of 1.5 percent. Again, take a few moments now to consider some places in your airport where you can form additional value.

How Do We Measure the Results of Key Organizational Interactions?

Just how do we measure the impact of Exceptionally Human communications? Human interactions are

Why Are We Doing This?

nebulous affairs. In one sense, there is no rigorously objective way to measure the impact of being an Exceptionally Human communicator — how do you stop or go back in time to find out? At the same time, we know the powerful downside of ineffective communication. The ASQ Survey is one tool to look at, including their new Employee Engagement Survey, as is the JD Power Airport Satisfaction Study. These respected and validated statistics can help guide us to discover specific areas to focus our communication efforts. We've all experienced the negativity that arises when confronted with ineffective communication practices — there are real costs associated with not communicating effectively. As we talked about a moment ago, envision what a 5 percent improvement in communication would look and feel like compared to those times when ineffective communication rules the exchange, and how that could result in a 5 percent difference in those ASQ and JD Power scores.

This is where we need to take a slight leap of faith and develop our own personal measurements. Do we notice improved workplace relationships, less frustration, greater camaraderie or increased happiness? You set the bar for yourself. Feel free to make adjustments anywhere along the way. The most important thing is to remain conscious, to seek out opportunities to be Exceptionally Human and to observe the results.

I would like to give you an example from my own professional experience, one that I think will help make these nebulous measurements less vague. This is about an airport that recognized their Value Zone and knew measuring results would be challenging. Nonetheless, they knew better communication strategies would have a significant impact on their people and customers.

A Case Study of Exceptionally Human Communications in The Value Zone

Annually, over 31 million travelers pass through Philadelphia International Airport. In September 2015, the airport was expecting a significant bump up in use, as the Catholic Church's tri-annual World Meeting of Families was coming to Philadelphia, and with it a visit by the extremely popular Pope Francis. Then, in 2016, the city would be hosting the Democratic National Convention, followed in 2017 by the NFL Draft.

The Airport's then-CEO, Mark Gale and his executive team, which included then-COO and now current CEO Chellie Cameron, recognized the importance of these events and the opportunity it presented the airport and the Philadelphia region. They recognized that the airport staff had a demanding job to perform under stressful conditions and that often they felt undervalued. They also recognized that the first and last interactions people have with the city are often at the airport and that those interactions have a significant positive or negative impact on how a city is perceived.

For Philadelphia, that means a city that has too often been defined by past events that were perceived more negatively than positively. It was an unprecedented opportunity for changing perceptions. Philadelphia had gone through some tough times, some rough years, but at this point the city was benefiting from a more than 10-year long renaissance. The Philadelphia of 2015 was a vastly different place than the Philadelphia of 1975, '85 or '95. Yet most people who aren't from the region, or haven't spent time there, tend to have an image of Philadelphia that lacks updated information. This was the city's and hence the airport's *ethos* or credibility issue.

Gale wanted to make sure all workers at PHL had the communication skills necessary to deliver an outstanding experience to those who passed through the airport, and for everyone to feel valued in the process. He wanted to establish the credibility of Philadelphia in travelers' minds. He wanted to create positive emotions in the visitors by creating positive emotions in staff. And he wanted to deliver the message that Philadelphia was a world-class city worth visiting, worth doing business in and holding conventions in, and the airport's workers were partners in delivering that message.

Like all airports, Gale had one more challenge. Of the 20,000 workers at PHL, slightly under 900 were employees of the airport itself and the other 19,000 worked for various agencies, including the TSA, state and federal agencies, and the airlines themselves. He had direct authority over just 4 percent of the actual airport workforce, even though he owned 100 percent of the responsibility for how the airport was perceived. So he had to be an Exceptionally Human communicator himself to get everyone to embrace his vision of Exceptional Human communication for airport visitors.

We sat down with Gale, Cameron and the rest of the executive team to pinpoint the airport's Value Zones, so as to best target a communication skill-building program that would allow workers to become Exceptionally Human communicators and assure travelers felt positively about their interactions. This established the foundation for *pathos*, or emotion. We knew the interactions between terminal personnel and passengers were important, but equally important were the interactions between management and those same personnel. As a result, we knew our work would have to be far reaching to have the impact we both desired, and it would include management as well as staff. Some Value Zones highlighted included interactions between custodial staff and travelers, airport administrators and stake-

Why Are We Doing This?

holder managers, frontline information booth personnel and travelers, as well as parking facility staff and customers.

So what did we do? We put into action the three elements of Exceptionally Human communications. We knew we needed to approach people from multiple agencies who did not often work together and get them all on the same page to create a similar value experience for travelers. To do this, we needed to establish credibility and trust. And to do that, we decided it was first necessary to make sure everyone attending these hospitality programs knew they were valued.

We began each program by listening. We asked participants to introduce themselves, let us know some additional personal information such as where they were born and how long they had worked at the airport. We wanted them to know we saw them as people first. Not only did we get a better sense of them, they got a better sense of each other. Trust was being developed on all fronts. We wanted them to listen to each other, to recognize the years of experience in the room, and to begin to forge relationships that would serve as the model for how they would interact with travelers and each other.

This foreshadowed the listening work that would come later. Gale and his executive team also wanted them to know how important they were. They wanted to give them skills to help them take care of themselves when under stress. We wanted them to feel cared for and to feel positive about their relationship with the airport. By stressing how this program was as much about helping them care for themselves as it was about caring for others, they began to feel valued, important and significant.

During the safety announcement on all flights, passengers are told to put their oxygen masks on first before assisting others; this is in essence what we were doing for the airport's personnel — putting them first. We were clear with them about the challenges of their positions, the stresses they would be under and that although they would see no financial reward if things went well, they would likely be blamed if things went wrong. We had an open and honest conversation about all of this, helping to build the trust and set the tone for the work ahead. We listened, we empathized and we were conscious to be Exceptionally Human with them, practicing what we were preaching. We let them know what skills they needed to develop and why. We gave them a reason and rationale for doing so in order to provide the *logos*, or the logic.

The most important issue that needed to be addressed was motivation. How were we going to get these employees motivated to develop the skills needed without having any true incentives to offer? Without addressing this question first, the entire training program would ultimately end in failure. So, we empathized. We let them tell of their experiences, of the difficulties of dealing with stressed-out people all the time and of the misplaced anger, frustration, and even aggressive behavior they are subjected to every day. We made certain that through our communication, by listening and giving our complete attention, they felt we were feeling what they were feeling. We made it clear that nobody expected them to suddenly change how they have been doing things; no one was asking them to make a 180-degree turn.

Instead, we asked them about the 5 percent rule, that if they practiced being Exceptionally Human communicators 5 percent more often than they currently did, what would it look like for *them*? And it was essential to let them know that there are indeed many times when they are exceptional. And that was key, keeping it focused on them and how the results would benefit them. Because if we kept focusing on the passengers, we ran the risk of having some of the most essential personnel feel overlooked, uncared for and isolated. So it had to be about them. And if they felt cared for, respected and understood, it significantly increased the chances they would do the same for the passengers they dealt with every day. We built credibility, we helped them feel positive about our interactions with them, and we reasonably pointed them in the right direction. We led by example so the Three Pillars of Exceptional Communication were put into action.

We knew there would be no simple way to measure the direct impact this program had. But Gale and his executive team knew the status quo would not be enough, so they took a well thought out leap of faith. They knew that if the airport's workforce would consciously practice being Exceptionally Human 5 percent more often, it would be well worth it, as a 5 percent increase in ASQ and/or JD Power scores significantly reflects how an airport is perceived. And the airport received significant local press coverage that highlighted the program. That in and of itself provided some direct, positive and unexpected feedback. In making the commitment, the ball started rolling.

Many people who came to Philadelphia for Pope Francis' visit, the Democratic National Convention and NFL Draft expressed happiness with their visit, experiences for which the airport can claim its reasonable fair share of the credit. And many people working at the airport told Gale and Cameron that the work had made a difference to them and that the effort carried over to their interactions with airport co-workers and travelers alike.

A Thought on Change: It's Easier Than You Think!

As humans, we are creatures of habit. We're less inclined to change because change can be scary. Change means things are going to be different. Change requires concerted effort. And, perhaps most of all, change can be uncomfortable. And being uncomfortable, even feeling perhaps a little pain, presents us with a challenge. Often any sign of discomfort or pain is seen as a problem and sends a signal that we should stop what we are doing so as to not make the discomfort worse. But there is a difference between good discomfort and bad discomfort.

An example of good discomfort is signaled by those sensations you feel the day after you start a new exercise routine. That soreness in your muscles causes you to ache in ways you never thought you could. There was a day back in high school, where I felt like I couldn't move after the first day of wrestling practice. If we take that discomfort as a signal to stop doing what we're doing, then we'll never get into the physical shape we desire and I would have never made the wrestling team. The same thing goes with learning to play guitar. Your fingertips will ache until you build up calluses and the pain ceases. But if you don't go through that discomfort, you'll never learn to play guitar. On the other hand, some activity can cause the bad discomfort. If after first working out, you feel a knife-like pain in your ankle every step you take, then you may want to stop what you are doing and consider calling a doctor. That's the bad discomfort, and that's what ultimately happened the first match of my senior season, ending my not-so-promising wrestling career.

So, as you begin navigating the road to becoming an Exceptionally Human communicator, understand it's not the mastery of these skills that's important, or even possible, but rather the continuous movement and effort toward mastery that matters. Take that pressure to be perfect off and put your energy into a simple and repetitive daily practice. As one of my tai chi instructors likes to light-heartedly say, "Practice won't necessarily make you perfect, but it will help you be a little less wrong." Sometimes, that's all we can ask for. So, when discomfort rears its head, ask yourself if this is something that needs to be endured or is it actively causing harm? Sometimes the answer may be easily apparent, but other times you may need to acquire more evidence before making a decision. One way or the other, you will feel some level of discomfort, so don't be surprised by it. Embrace the discomfort, transform it and savor the reward. Easier said than done, I know, yet that perseverance and effort is well worth it.

Parting Thoughts: Exceptionally Human Airports

Being human is to be filled with emotions, thoughts, expectations and desires. Being human is to be impacted by the environment around us as we simultaneously impact that environment. Airports are vast spaces where human beings interact, connect and assist one another; they are intrinsically human and emotionally filled spaces. As ASQ's Dimitri Coll stated in this book's forward, the entire airport experience is an emotional one. Because of this, the entire range of human emotions is present at airports, whether or not they are fully expressed. Air travel has become increasingly stressful with crowded airplanes, grumpy people, security concerns, terrorist threats, significant weather events and other assorted incidents that can bring out less-than-desirable behaviors; humanity is on full display at airports. They are one of the few places where class, race, gender, religion and nationality all intersect with a common goal — to get from point A to point B. Airports are a rich tapestry of human experience, a well of potential value just waiting to be extracted with the right tools and techniques. And in spite of all the technology that has allowed airports to enhance and expedite the travel experience, at the end of the day airports are about people and the emotional complexities that define them.

I define Exceptionally Human as that state or condition in which the interactions between people is one where all involved feel their experience is validated and valued and there's an implicit acknowledgment of what each person brings to that interaction. Exceptionally Human is a desired state, a point to aspire to and a condition that is mutually created, though it may require more effort from one party than it does from another. Being Exceptionally Human means bringing a conscious awareness to any particular interaction so communication can be adjusted and the most value can be derived from it. It requires effort and may not always hit the mark, but it will leave an impression that the interaction mattered.

An Exceptionally Human Airport is a place where human beings come together and experience a sense of well being, feeling valued, and worth that helps to facilitate an outstanding experience for all those who move within an airport's borders. An Exceptionally Human Airport is a place where investments are made to cultivate and advance the communication practices of all those who work there, for it is the interactions that take place between human beings that most greatly shape the airport experience.

Each and every airport is already Exceptionally Human in its own unique way, so no airport is starting from scratch. At the same time, each and every airport has ways in which its communication can be enhanced so as to be that much more Exceptionally Human for the people who work there and travel through it.

If an airport is to become as Exceptionally Human as it can be, it must focus on the people who work there and empower them with the skills necessary to create the best experience possible. Communication is the key. Communication is what allows people to be exceptional with one another. Communication is what allows authentic connections to be made. Communication allows people to successfully share their experience and serve one another. It allows people to understand the needs of one another and meet those needs. Without fully developed communication skills, money is essentially left on the table, as the exceptional value latent in each and every airport interaction remains dormant — the tools required to extract that value aren't there. Effective communication allows people to experience the sense of being valued. In his article "Feeling Valued Will Boost Morale, Motivate and Encourage Future Input," Smitha Syed Ali pointed out that this input is critical in increasing levels of employee engagement at airports.

An Exceptionally Human Airport is one in which

> *Communication is what allows people to be exceptional with one another.*

positive experiences are shaped and negative experiences transformed, or at the very least minimized. Exceptionally Human Airports are places where people actually enjoy going to because they are spaces that value their own unique humanness. Exceptionally Human Airports are places where people enjoy working. Exceptionally Human Airports become the place on a traveler's journey where they know they can take a deep breath and let their guard down, because they know the people at the airport will take care of them.

Becoming an Exceptionally Human Airport is a process. It requires some serious inquiries into how the airport workforce is being treated. It requires looking beyond the barriers that can exist between stakeholder organizations, so everyone at the airport knows they are an integral part of the airport experience. It requires expanding ownership and expanding influence. Most importantly, it requires an ability to strategically and thoughtfully communicate to a vast audience composed of countless personalities, so people know they are valued. If there are two words that best sum up the Exceptionally Human Airport Experience, those words would be, "Feeling valued!"

Communication Skills Appendix

There are three key skills to help your airport become an even more Exceptionally Human airport. Here they are...

Listening

Chances are, in the course of your education, no matter the level completed, we all had to take math, English, science, and some type of history class. Chances are also high that we never took a class called listening. Now it's quite possible that listening was incorporated into another class, but that's not the same as having a class dedicated entirely to listening. I can tell you from my experience teaching classes in 20 different colleges and universities across the United States in Communication Studies, a field dedicated to researching the how and why of human communication, only one school offered a class called "Listening" (that was Cabrillo College in Aptos, California). Think about that for a minute. Of the vital skills we develop in our lives, listening has to rank up there in the top 3. And for some reason, nobody bothered to teach us how to do it. So, as a result, we learn on the fly, which usually is good enough, but good enough will not take us to great. And if we are in any way going to become the Exceptionally Human communicators we want to be, we need to begin by becoming better listeners.

Listening is a skill, and like any skill, be it playing a musical instrument, cooking, swimming, or dancing, we need to learn how to do it properly followed by practice, practice, and more practice. One of the reasons we haven't been taught how to listen is because if our ears function properly, if we can hear, then the assumption is that we are listening. Well, that's like saying just because we can press down the keys on a piano we are considered a concert pianist. The two are distinctly different things, as one is something that requires little effort and the other requires hours of dedicated practice to master. This is not to say we all need to now dedicate endless hours to develop our listening prowess, although it would be helpful, but this is about truly recognizing the distinctions between hearing and listening so we will know what we need to actually do to develop this vital skill.

First thing to recognize is that hearing is an involuntary response to stimuli, whereas listening is an active exercise in engagement. Hearing is effortless. We do not need to expend excessive energy to hear. If you've ever tried to go to sleep while traffic is roaring outside your window, you can attest to the fact that hearing happens, like it or not. Listening, however, requires effort, as effective listening involves more than simply **hearing**, it also involves **attending, understanding, responding,** and **remembering**. These five things constitute listening.

We've already covered hearing. **Attending** is actually paying attention to what is being communicated, being present and focused on what is being communicated as well as how it is being communicated. That means avoiding distractions and staying present with the other person, an increasingly difficult task in our on-demand age. **Understanding** is just that, making sure that what was communicated is something we understand, and if we don't understand it, we let the other person know so they can help achieve understanding. Don't nod in agreement or say you understand if you don't, because when you do you've technically stopped listening. **Responding** is providing the person who is communicating with us a sign that we are actually present with them. Whether a nodding head, a smile, or an emoji, it lets the other person know we are there with them. Finally, to truly have fully listened, we need to be able to recall what the other person has communicated; we need to **remember**. Now, we're not going to remember all things at all times, as we are human, but to be that Exceptionally Human listener, we need to take steps necessary to assure we can remember, like taking notes. It's only when we've heard, attended, understood, responded, and remembered, that we can say we have listened. Like I said, no simple task, but certainly one worth investing our time and energy to develop.

It's worth pointing out that there are very legitimate barriers to effective listening. I've already touched upon the fact we haven't been taught to listen. Other barriers include information overload, being distracted, not feeling well, competing thoughts, and fatigue are but a few. Simply recognize that we're not going to wake up tomorrow and magically become listening superstars. We need to make a concerted effort to listen, to block out distractions and dedicate ourselves to doing the 5 things required to listen. That's why I like the 5% rule. We're not going to be that exceptionally human listener all the time, but if we can make that concerted effort 5% more often, 24 more workday minutes than we do now, then we won't be putting too much pressure on ourselves and we'll go a long way in that direction.

By becoming a better listener, you will stand out and be noticed. People like being listened to (they may actually be taken aback because it is so unusual). Listening enables us to find the deeper meaning behind the words people use, which is 90% or more of what constitutes communication. Listening allows us to develop strong connections with the people we communicate with, as people value people who listen to them. Listening builds that vital trust, increases your credibility, and people feel positively about their exchanges with us. Listening provides us with the insights that allow us to understand what others find rational, logical, and reasonable. Listening provides us with the insights that allow us to be a more competent communicator.

Empathy

What is empathy? Ask this question to someone on the street or at work and the answer might be understanding or knowing what someone else is feeling. And with that answer, you'll be halfway to empathy. The other, and even more important half, would include feeling what someone else is feeling. As a matter of fact, you could even dispose of the first half and simply define empathy as feeling what another person is feeling. That is what empathy truly is. And what's nice, is that as human beings, we are hard-wired to empathize, and at times it's an almost reflexive act. When you watch someone giving a presentation and it's clear from their delivery that they are extremely nervous, you start to feel nervous as well. That's because you are empathizing with them, feeling what they are feeling. When you watch movies, you get into the characters emotions, and that's also the power of empathy (thanks to those mirror neurons in our brains). There are notable exceptions, such as people with narcissistic personality disorder or sociopaths, but for a vast majority of people, empathy is as natural as breathing.

But just because it's natural, doesn't mean that we always do it, and that in fact, there are countless other times when empathy requires tremendous focused effort. We can be so overcome by our own experiences, our own feelings, by stress and fatigue, that our ability to empathize becomes significantly compromised. Again, at an airport this is especially true.

One significant challenge to empathy is taking our own emotional experience and placing it second, and placing the other person's emotional state first. Empathy demands that we put aside whatever it is we may be feeling so we can feel what another person is feeling. And that's no simple task, especially when we are experiencing rather charged emotions, such as anger, disappointment, or fear, as they tend to take us over completely. However, when we can move beyond what we are feeling, we can make the effort to, however briefly, step outside ourselves, we can gain valuable insights into the other person, insights that will inform the choices we make when we communicate with them in order to better connect with them. When we feel what someone else is feeling, and we are being Exceptionally

Human communicators, other people will notice, because in this stress filled, rapidly changing, iWorld we live in, empathy has taken a back seat. More often than not, people are empathizing less often, through no fault of their own. Fortunately, with a little effort, it need not remain that way, and that is another big step towards being an Exceptionally Human airport.

Breathing

Modern life is stressful and stress has a significant impact on our thinking and communication behaviors. Typically when under stress, our brains will go into fight or flight mode; we will either confront the stress with aggression or hostility, or we will move away from or avoid the situation. Our breathing gets shallow as our bodies prepare to defend/attack or flee, and our capacity to engage in more meaningful communication practices becomes compromised, as blood is diverted from our brains and redistributed to other vital body organs. Our bodies seem to be hard-wired to have these stress responses, and although helpful in truly life-threatening situations, they can have significant downsides in terms of our communication and the negative impact it has on others. We must find a way to work with stress so it does not work against us.

What is interesting is that when we are under

physical stress, such as running or biking, our bodies respond in ways that allow us to overcome the stress in a positive manner. Our muscles are working harder, and as a result need additional oxygen. The way our muscles acquire oxygen is through the blood, so our breathing unconsciously deepens, more air enters our lungs, more oxygen enters our bloodstream, and feeds our stressed muscles. Perfect.

When we are under mental stress, however, our bodies respond in a way that makes it more difficult to overcome the stress in a positive manner. Our brains are working harder, and as a result, need additional oxygen. But instead of our breath deepening, our breathing becomes much more shallow, and we are in effect denying our bodies the one thing it needs to work more effectively, oxygen. As a result, our decision making capacity becomes compromised as the fight or flight response tightens its grip. To counteract this tendency, and to bring more blood flow and oxygen to our brains, we need to become conscious of our breathing.

I would like to focus on two types of breathing we engage in. The first is called **thoracic breathing**. Thoracic breathing is the shallow breathing we use almost all day long. We are drawing air into our lungs via our mouths, and as a result tend to only use the top 10% of our lung capacity, bringing in just enough oxygen so all systems are functioning well. And when we are under stress, our thoracic breathing, which is already shallow to begin with, gets that much more shallow. As a result, we are bringing less oxygen into our lungs, which means less oxygen into our blood, which means less oxygen into our brain.

Diaphragmatic breathing, on the other hand, is a deeper breathing practice that starts at the diaphragm, which lies just below our lungs. This breathing is best accessed via our nose, and we draw air much deeper into our lungs, almost like filling up a glass of water from the bottom to the top. As a result, we bring much more oxygen into our lungs, that gets transferred into our blood, and distributed to our brain and other vital organs. Whereas thoracic breathing requires little conscious effort, diaphragmatic breathing requires focused effort.

Here's a simple diaphragmatic breathing exercise you can practice so when stressful circumstances arise, you will be prepared to bring the much needed oxygen to your brain, so our Exceptionally Human communication practices can thrive.

1. Sit upright in your chair, spine straight, feet flat on the ground, hands resting comfortably on your thighs, eyes open.
2. Slowly exhale completely through your mouth, making sure your keep your spine straight.
3. Slowly, to a count of 5, gently inhale through

you nose, engaging your diaphragm as you fill your lungs up with air from the bottom up to the top, like a glass being filled with water. (Note how your chest will rise as you do this.)
4. Once your lungs are full, hold for ½ second, then slowly and gently exhale to a count of 5, either through your nose or mouth, being certain to keep your spine straight so as to avoid collapsing your chest. (Note this is not a rapid exhale, but a controlled exhale.)
5. Once you've exhaled completely, inhale again (step 3), and then exhale (step 4).
6. Repeat 5 times in a row, 2-3 times a day, for 3 weeks.

References

Barsade, S. G. (2002). The ripple effect: emotional contagion and its influence on group behavior. *Administrative Science Quarterly*, 47(4), 644+.

Barton, Byron (1982). *Airport*. New York: Harper Collins.

Bogart, A. (2001). *A director prepares: seven essays on art and theatre*. London: Routledge.

Botsman, R. (2017). *Who can you trust? how technology brought us together and why it might drive us apart*. New York: Hachette.

Burleson, B. & Caplan, S. (1998). *Cognitive complexity. Communication and Personality: Trait Perspectives*.

Catlette, B., & Hadden, R. (2012). *Contented cows still give better milk: the plain truth about employee engagement and your bottom line*. 2nd ed. Hoboken, N.J.: John Wiley & Sons.

Cooper, L. (1932). *The rhetoric of aristotle*. London: Prentice Hall.

Cotton, B. (2007). The modern airport, conquering complexity in an era of increasing expectations. *A Frost & Sullivan white paper, document #TTW030007-USEN-00.*

Drusch, M., Lees, E., & Freibrun, S. (2017, Oct). Reimagining the passenger experience: the importance of airport and airline collaboration. *Airport Business*, 12-15.

Ellis, A (2001). *Overcoming destructive beliefs, feelings, and behaviors: new directions for rational emotive behavior Therapy.* Amherst, New York; Prometheus.

Fodness, D., & Murray, B. (2007). Passengers' expectations of airport service quality. *The Journal of Services Marketing*, 21(7), 492-506.

Francis, G., Humphreys, I., & Fry, J., (2002). The benchmarking of airport performance. *Journal of Air Transport Management*, 8, 239-247.

Gottman, J. S., & Gottman, J. (2015, Nov). Lessons from the love lab. *Psychotherapy Networker*, 39.

Graham, A. (2008). How important are commercial revenues to today's airports? *Journal of Air Transport Management*, 15(3), 1 – 6.

Gupta, R., & Venkaiah, V. (2015). Airport passengers: Their needs and satisfaction. *SCMS Journal of Indian Management*, 12(3), 46-57.

Heskett, J. L., Jones, T. O., Loveman, G. W., Sasser, W. E., Jr., & Schlesinger, L. A. (1994). Putting the service-profit chain to work. *Harvard Business Review*, 72(2), 164+.

Hill, L., Brandeau, G., Truelove, E. & Lineback, K. (2014). *Collective genius: the art of practice and leading innovation*. Boston: Harvard Business Review Press.

Humphreys, I., & Francis, G. (2002). Performance measurement: a review of airports. *International Journal of Transport Management*, 1(2), 79-85.

Hunter, J. A., & Lambert, J. R. (2016). Do we feel safer today? the impact of smiling customer service on airline safety perception post 9-11. *Journal of Transportation Security*, 9(1-2), 35-56.

Littlejohn, S. W. (1999). *Theories of human communication*. Belmont, CA: Wadsworth.

Maidenberg, M. (2017, July 18). United airlines profits rise despite boycott threats over passenger treatment. *New York Times*, p. B5.

Nayar, V. (2010). *Employees first, customers second*. Boston: Harvard Business Press.

O'Connor, M. & Dornfeld, B. (2014). *The moment you can't ignore*. New York: Public Affairs.

Parasuraman, A., Zeithaml, V. A., & Berry, L. L. (1988). SERVQUAL: A multiple-item scale for measuring consumer perceptions of service quality. *Journal of Retailing*, 64(1), 12.

Park, J. & Jung, S. (2011), "Transfer passengers' perceptions of airport service quality: a case study of incheon international airport", *International Business Research*, 4(3), 75-82.

Paternoster, J. (2007). Excellent airport customer service meets successful branding strategy. *Airport Management*, 2(3): 218-226.

Pennebaker, J. (2011). *The secret life of pronouns: what our words say about us*. New York: Bloomsbury.

Rahman, Z. (2004). Developing Customer Oriented Service: A Case Study. *Managing Service Quality*, 14(5), 426-435.

Schaberg, C. (2016). *The end of airports*. New York: Bloomsbury.

Scott, K. (2017). London city airport offers benefits to increase employees' financial confidence. *Employee Benefits*.

Smitha, S. A. (2013). A study on employee engagement in cochin international airport limited. *Drishtikon: A Management Journal*, 4(1), 24-47.

Spitzberg, B. H, & Cupach, W. R. (1984). *Interpersonal communication competence*. Beverly Hills: Sage Publications.

Straker, K., & Wrigley, C. (2016). Translating emotional insights into digital channel designs. *Journal of Hospitality and Tourism Technology*, 7(2), 135-157.

Subha, M. V., & Archana, R. (2013). Identifying the dimensions of service quality as antecedents to passenger satisfaction of rajiv gandhi international airport. *Journal of Contemporary Research in Management*, 8(2), 25-33.

Surachartkumtonkun, J., Patterson, P. G., & McColl-Kennedy, J. (2013). Customer rage back-story: Linking needs-based cognitive appraisal to service failure type. *Journal of Retailing*, 89(1), 72-87.

Other Resources

Grant, A. (2013). *Give and take*. New York: Penguin Group.

Hurst, A.(2014). *The purpose economy*. Boise, ID: Elevate.

Moon, Y. (2010). *Different: escaping the competitive herd*. New York: Crown Business.

Pink, D. H. (2009). *Drive: the surprising truth about what motivates us*. New York: Penguin, 2009.

Winner, M. G. & Crooke, P. (2011). *Social thinking at work: why should I care?* San Jose, CA: Think Social Publishing.

About the Author

Brian Shapiro is a dynamic communication professional, author, and keynote speaker with 20+ years experience in consulting, training, higher education, and the performing arts. Brian has helped thousands of individuals enhance and improve their workplace communication in industries that include the airport, technology, transportation, hospitality, government and nonprofit sectors. An affiliated faculty member at The University of Pennsylvania, he is the founder and president of Shapiro Communications, a professional development company providing workplace communication workshops and training programs that produce the healthiest customer, client, and employee experiences possible. Brian attended a doctorate program in Performance Studies at The University of Texas at Austin, and holds a BA (San Diego State University) and MA (San Francisco State University) in Communication Studies. A dedicated tai chi and yoga practitioner, Brian's written and performed in numerous original theatrical productions and is the vocalist/lyricist for the Paris-based musical trio, Grand Plateau. Born and raised in California, Brian and his family currently live in Philadelphia.

About Shapiro Communications

Shapiro Communications is a professional development company providing workplace communication workshops and training programs with a distinctly human touch. Since 2010, Shapiro Communications has helped thousands of individuals in the airport, transportation, technology, and hospitality sectors enhance their communication in areas such as customer happiness, employee enthusiasm, professional presentations, and avoiding unintended offenses and slights. A proud member of ACI-NA and AAAE, Shapiro Communications is dedicated to ensuring their client's communication in the workplace produces the healthiest customer, client, and employee experiences possible.

For more information about Shapiro Communications, visit **www.shapirocommunications.com**

Phone: 215.805.1695

Email: info@shapirocommunications.com

Mailing address:
245 S. 16th Street
Philadelphia, PA 19102

Made in the USA
Columbia, SC
06 April 2018